HAL LEONARD ACCORDION METHOD

BY BEVERLY GRACE JOY

PLAYBACK+
Speed • Pitch • Balance • Loop

To access audio visit:
www.halleonard.com/mylibrary

Enter Code
7806-5068-3477-7241

Cover photo courtesy of Victoria Accordions

ISBN 978-1-5400-1266-1

Visit Hal Leonard Online at
www.halleonard.com

Contact us:
Hal Leonard
7777 West Bluemound Road
Milwaukee, WI 53213
Email: info@halleonard.com

In Europe, contact:
Hal Leonard Europe Limited
42 Wigmore Street
Marylebone, London, W1U 2RN
Email: info@halleonardeurope.com

In Australia, contact:
Hal Leonard Australia Pty. Ltd.
4 Lentara Court
Cheltenham, Victoria, 3192 Australia
Email: info@halleonard.com.au

CONTENTS

INTRODUCTION

Welcome to a new *Accordion Method* developed for you!

Designed to introduce the beginning student to the diverse potential of this versatile musical instrument, this method presents innovative approaches not offered in most beginner accordion methods:

1. The C position, which has dominated both accordion and piano beginner methods – and has frequently obstructed learning to read notes – will not characterize the earliest learning in this method. Rather, students will be challenged to read notes without false finger associations, which have been the downfall of developing correct reading concepts when the old approach has been used.

2. Students will be introduced to the entire right-hand keyboard with consecutive five-finger patterns and combine this with left-hand buttons, F C G D A E. This orients students to the relationship between the alphabetical system of the right-hand keyboard and the intervallic arrangement based on fifths of the left-hand button fundamental row.

3. Early development of facility in reading and playing bass-button notes, including five counterbasses, eight fundamental basses, major, minor, and seventh chords.

4. Varied and musically satisfying accompaniment and bass solo patterns. This is vital so the right hemisphere of the brain (which directs left-hand activity) is stimulated to develop, even as the right-hand (left hemisphere) facility grows. Earlier preponderance and almost exclusive use of "bass-chord-chord" patterns has stymied right-hemisphere development – an unhappy disservice to students. Left-hand fingerings will be varied, logical, and contextual, just as the right hand has logical fingerings for ease.

5. Teaching several meters and rhythms includes learning to conduct while counting, tapping while counting rhythmic exercises, reading and counting with graphic proportional symbols that provide visual representations of longer and shorter (proportional) note values.

6. Guidance for pulling (⊓) and pushing (∨) bellows. These symbols – down-bow and up-bow indications – are borrowed from the literature of the string family of musical instruments.

TO PLAY OR TO PRACTICE...

All too often, lessons and learning amount to practicing only, so that for all the effort, one never is able to enjoy the fruit of one's labor. As you progress through this book, be sure to retain a list of early pieces you have learned. Review these pieces (while learning new pieces) until you can actually enjoy playing them. This list should be updated from time to time, so that newer (but-now-older) learned pieces can be played for enjoyment (even shared with friends or family) while you are practicing and/or getting acquainted with more complex pieces.

ABOUT THE AUTHOR

Beverly Grace Joy has an extensive musical background in accordion, piano, composition, theory, and pedagogy. Beverly spent her early years as a contest-winning accordionist (Iowa State Accordion Contest – performing at the Chicagoland Music Festival at age 16, followed by winning first in the American Accordionists Association National Contest, first in the senior division of the Wisconsin State Accordion Contest, first in the Accordion Teachers Guild National competitions in 1962, which led to participation in the Coupe Mondiale in Baden-Baden, Germany.) She proceeded to earn a Bachelor of Music Education in piano and a Master of Music in Theory and Composition, also completing piano study and a recital under Dr. Kenneth Drake for a Piano Master in the College of Fine Arts at Drake University. She was a national winner in the National Conference on Piano Pedagogy Composition Competition, having the winning compositions published. Following a teaching career in several colleges and universities in the intervening years, she has maintained a studio in her home for the past 25 years and has published several pieces for piano as well as a unique, innovative beginning piano method.

LESSON 1
GETTING ACQUAINTED WITH YOUR ACCORDION

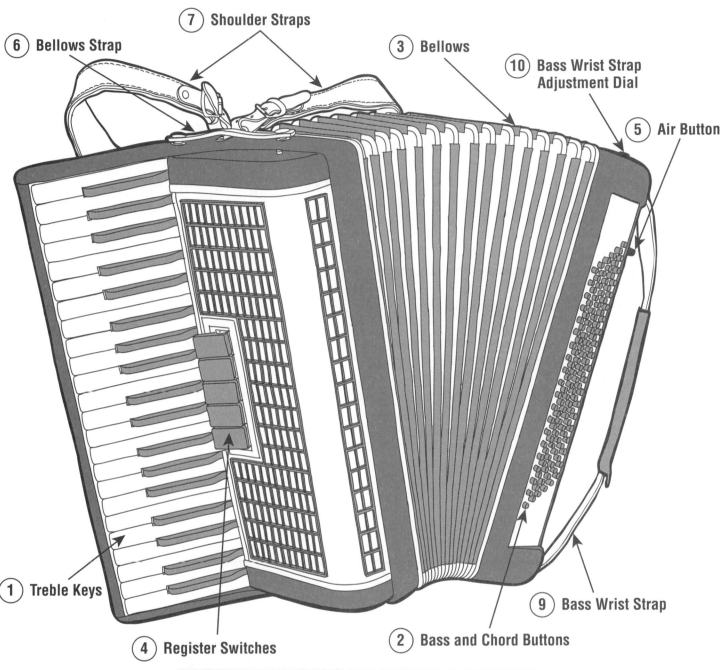

⑦ **Shoulder Straps**

⑥ **Bellows Strap**

③ **Bellows**

⑩ **Bass Wrist Strap Adjustment Dial**

⑤ **Air Button**

① **Treble Keys**

④ **Register Switches**

② **Bass and Chord Buttons**

⑨ **Bass Wrist Strap**

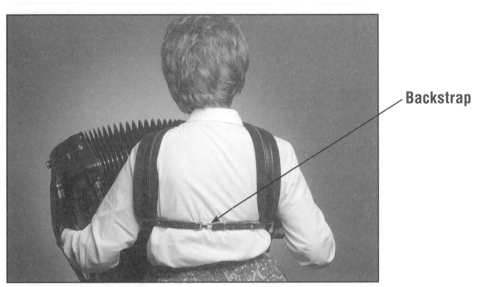

Backstrap

1. **Treble Keys:** Perhaps you have noticed that the black keys are arranged in alternating sets of three and two keys. This makes the white keys keyboard easy to learn. First, the easiest white key to locate is the D key, which is between every set of two black keys. There are three Ds on your keyboard. Nearest to your chin are the first two white keys, F and G, followed by A B C. These lead to the first **D**, followed by E F G. Next, there are two more consecutive sets of A B C **D** E F G and A B C **D** E F G, plus the highest-sounding key A (which is actually nearest to the floor). So, the white keys, starting just below your chin, are F G, A B C **D** E F G, A B C **D** E F G, A B C **D** E F G, A.

2. **Bass and Chord Buttons:** A 120-Bass accordion has six rows of twenty buttons. The row nearest the bellows is named the Counterbass row, while the second row from the bellows is the Fundamental Bass row. The other four rows have chords.

3. **Bellows:** Accordionists are really wind players, similarly to clarinetists, bassoonists, et al. Just as a clarinetist blows air between a reed and mouthpiece while fingering different places to make the varied pitches, the accordionist, as he/she presses the different keys and buttons, pushes air with the bellows to activate the reeds (opened by the keys and/or buttons) that produce the many accordion pitches.

4. **Register Switches:** These switches open and close sets of reeds to change the sound or octave.

5. **Air Button:** With this button depressed, you can open or close the bellows silently.

6. **Bellows Straps:** These should always be fastened when the instrument is not in use and whenever it is stored in the case, to avoid damaging your accordion as you move it about and in and out of the case.

7. **Shoulder Straps:** Shoulder straps should be adjusted for stability and comfort.

8. **Back Strap:** The back strap is essential to maintain this stability and comfort. It comes in two parts that are attached to each shoulder strap and fastens together halfway down the back.

9. **Bass Wrist Strap:** The bass strap supports your wrist and arm as you pull and push the bellows.

10. **Adjustment Dial:** The adjustment dial allows you to set your own comfort/support position for the bass wrist strap.

THE GRAND STAFF

Accordionists, like pianists, read music on the **grand staff**. Notes for the right hand are written on the treble clef, and notes for the left hand are written on the bass clef.

lower tones near the chin

The accordion keyboard has 41 keys:
24 white and 17 black.

higher tones near the knee

F G A B C D E F G A B C D E F G A B C D E F G A

LESSON 2

PLAYING THE TREBLE KEYBOARD

There are several ways to move around the treble keyboard. One is simply to move your hand to a new place. We will learn that first. There are seven different alphabetical keys (A B C D E F G) on the treble, but you have only five fingers, so we will play five-key sets using fingers 1-2-3-4-5.

Get to know your finger numbers: Practice tapping fingers of both hands, saying twice:

- "Thumbs – One" (repeat)
- "Pointer – Two"
- "Tall Man – Three"
- "Ring Man – Four"
- "Pinkie – Five"

PRACTICING RULES: Always begin slowly. If that doesn't work, study the lesson again and go MORE SLOWLY. Everything should be practiced a dozen times at each practice session (unless it needs more, or you are just enjoying your success). Three times doesn't cut it! ONLY CORRECT PLAYING COUNTS AS PRACTICE. If accidents happen (and they might once in awhile, since this is a rather sophisticated, new skill you are learning), these are categorized as "throw-away experiments" – and that's okay; they just don't count as practice. After all, why would we want to "practice" incorrectly?

Near your chin, put your thumb (1) on the first F key, then, play and say "F G A B C" in order, using fingers 1 2 3 4 5.

Next, replace the fifth finger on C with your thumb (1) on C. Now, play/say "C D E F G" in order, using fingers 1 2 3 4 5.

Now replace the fifth finger on G with your thumb (1) on G. Now, play/say "G A B C D" in order, using fingers 1 2 3 4 5. Continue playing/saying key-name sets to the top of the keyboard.

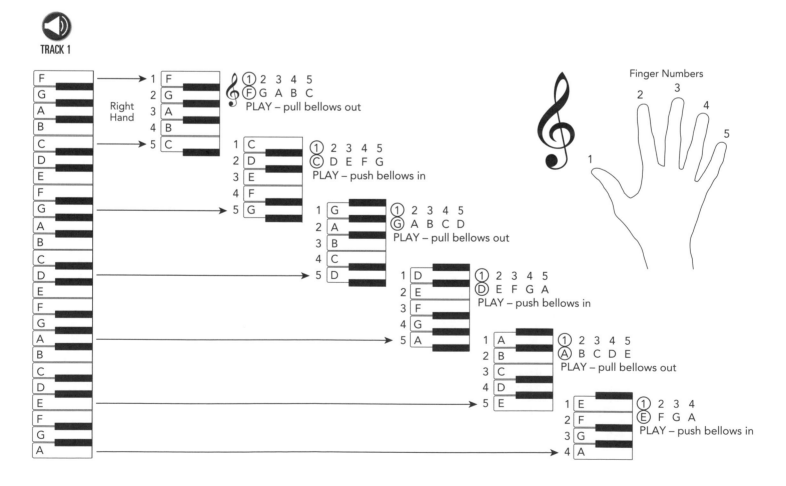

PLAYING THE BASS BUTTONS

Insert your left hand through the bass strap. It should fit snugly. Use the bass strap adjustment dial to change the strap length if necessary.

To begin: Near the center of the fundamental row locate the C bass button with your third finger. The C bass button has either a rhinestone or a depression* for ease in locating it.

TRACK 2

Now, follow these steps: (Find the bass buttons below in the fundamental bass row.)

1. Move the third finger down (toward your knee) to the F bass button. Play the F button saying "F." pull bellows

2. Move the third finger up (toward your head) to the C button. Play and say "C." push

3. Move the third finger up to the G button. Play and say "G." pull

4. Move the third finger up to the D button. Play and say "D." push

5. Move the third finger up to the A button. Play and say "A." pull

6. Move the third finger up to the E button. Play and say "E." push

Also, practice this exercise using the fourth finger of the left hand, then with the second finger.

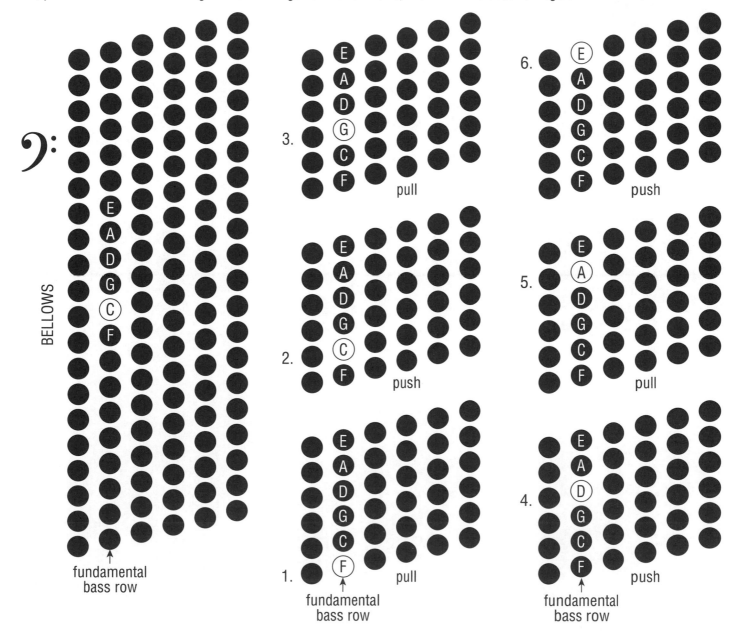

*If your accordion does not have a depression or any identifying mark on the E bass button, ask an accordion repairman to put a mark on the E button as well as the A♭ button. (These buttons are four above and four below the C button.)

PLAYING TREBLE KEYBOARD AND BASS BUTTONS COMBINED

Study Column 1. On the treble keyboard find the F key, just below your chin, with your right-hand thumb. Keep your thumb there. Now, find the F button in the fundamental row of basses with your left-hand finger 3.

Pull the bellows out as you play both Fs at the same time with both hands, and hold the F button of the left hand while you play the remaining four keys of the treble (G A B C).

Next, study Column 2. Move your right-hand thumb to the C key and stay there. Move up to the C button with left-hand finger 3. Push bellows in, play both Cs at the same time with both hands, and hold the C button of the left hand while you play the remaining four keys of the treble (D E F G).

Study Column 3. Move your right-hand thumb to the G key; stay there. Move up to the G button with left-hand finger 3. Pull the bellows out, play both Gs at the same time, and hold the G button of the left hand while you play the remaining four keys of the treble (A B C D).

TRACK 3

COLUMN 1	COLUMN 2	COLUMN 3

 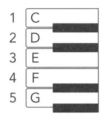 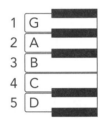

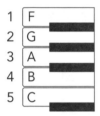

	1	2	3	4	5
	F	G	A	B	C

PLAY

F (hold - - -)
3 (pull bellows out)

	1	2	3	4	5
	C	D	E	F	G

PLAY

C (hold - - -)
3 (push bellows in)

	1	2	3	4	5
	G	A	B	C	D

PLAY

G (hold - - -)
3 (pull bellows out)

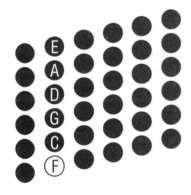

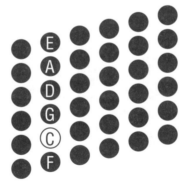

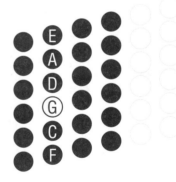

Continue moving up the treble keyboard (actually *down* toward the floor). On this page, (see column 4), your right-hand thumb will play D, the thirteenth key from your chin, followed by E F G A. In column 5, the right-hand thumb will play A, followed by B C D E. Finally, (column 6) the right-hand thumb plays the highest-sounding E, followed by F G A. Your left-hand finger 3 will continue moving up one button, first D (see Column 4), then A (see Column 5), and finally E (see Column 6).

Repeat pages 10 and 11, first use finger 4 of your left hand on the buttons (F C G D A E), repeat and use finger 2 of your left hand on the buttons.

COLUMN 4

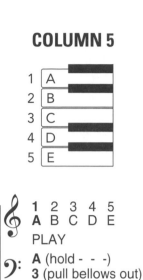

1 2 3 4 5
D E F G A
PLAY
D (hold - - -)
3 (push bellows in)

COLUMN 5

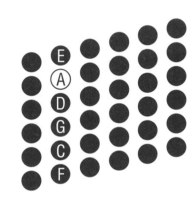

1 2 3 4 5
A B C D E
PLAY
A (hold - - -)
3 (pull bellows out)

COLUMN 6

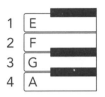

1 2 3 4
E F G A
PLAY
E (hold - - -)
3 (push bellows in)

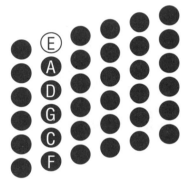

LESSON 3

TIME FOR ACTION

On the next several pages, there are two familiar melodies you will play, first with the right hand and later with both hands (using bass buttons to accompany these melodies). You will play these tunes in several places on the keyboard and buttons.

First, with the third/tall finger, locate the E key (the seventh key counting from your chin). Arrange the other fingers around this E key (1 on C, 2 on D, 3 on E, 4 on F, and 5 on G). Follow the finger numbers and key names below to play this well-known melody. These signs (⊓ = PULL, V = PUSH) tell you when to pull out and push in the bellows as you play.

Now, move your third/tall finger to the next E key. Counting from the E key you just played, move up (actually down toward the floor) to the 14th white key, which is also E. This is called playing an octave higher. Play as before, again arranging fingers 1 on C, 2 on D, 3 on E, 4 on F, 5 on G, and listen to this melody in a range that a flute player would use. Next, move up to the highest E, the 21st white key, and you may sound like a piccolo player.

TRACK 4

ODE TO JOY

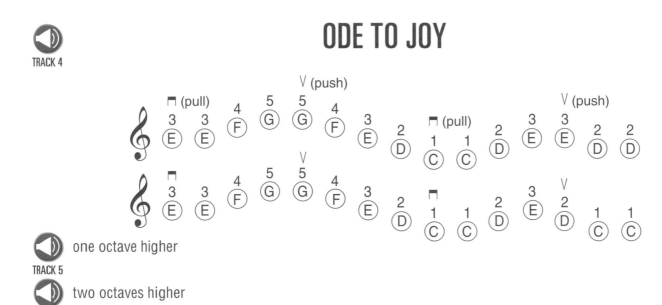

one octave higher
TRACK 5
two octaves higher
TRACK 6

Next, we will transpose, which means you will play in a different place from C D E F G. Transposing this melody is easy. Professional musicians often transpose music for a variety of reasons. So, again with your third/tall finger, find the fourth key from your chin, the B key. Arrange your fingers with 1 on G, 2 on A, 3 on B, 4 on C, and 5 on D. Now, play this piece in this new place. This transposed version can also be moved an octave (3rd finger on the 11th key, B), as well as two octaves (3rd finger on the 18th key, B), higher. Try it!

TRACK 7

ODE TO JOY

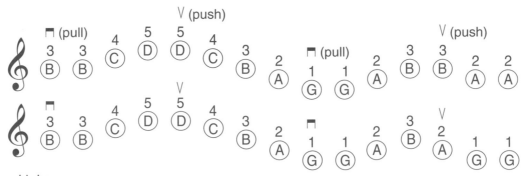

one octave higher
TRACK 8
two octaves higher
TRACK 9

BASS BUTTONS WARM-UPS

To prepare for the next several pages, we will play some easy warm-ups, using just four bass buttons (F, C, G, and D) in pairs (C with G, G with D, and F with C).

TRACK 10

1. Practice the left-hand third finger on C and second finger on G as indicated:

$\mathbf{9}\colon$ | PULL **C** (HOLD) 3   PUSH **G** (HOLD) 2   PULL **C** (HOLD) 3   PUSH **G** (HOLD) 2   (play 3 times)

TRACK 11

2. Practice G and D with the left-hand third and second fingers.

$\mathbf{9}\colon$ | PULL **G** (HOLD) 3   PUSH **D** (HOLD) 2   PULL **G** (HOLD) 3   PUSH **D** (HOLD) 2   (play 3 times)

TRACK 12

3. Practice F and C with the left-hand third and second fingers.

$\mathbf{9}\colon$ | PULL **F** (HOLD) 3   PUSH **C** (HOLD) 2   PULL **F** (HOLD) 3   PUSH **C** (HOLD) 2   (play 3 times)

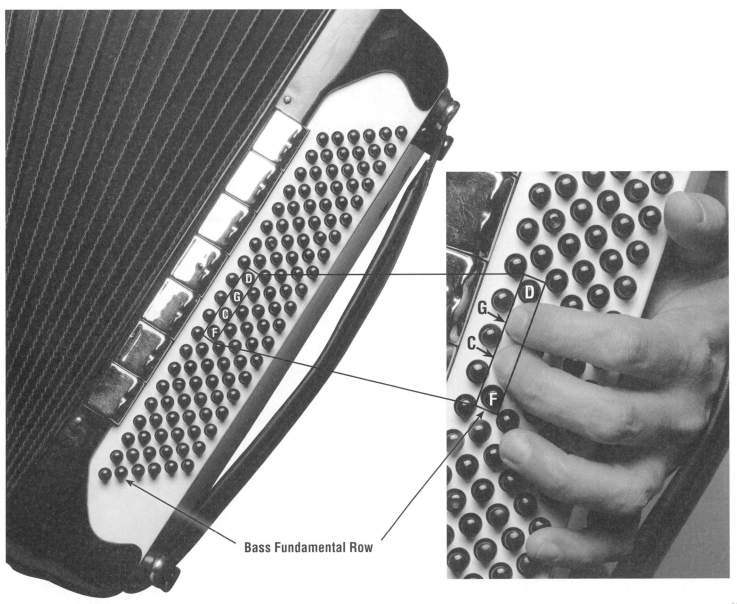

Bass Fundamental Row

TIME FOR ACTION WITH BOTH HANDS AT ONCE

Note: Whether reading and playing right-hand alone or both hands ($\flat$) and ($\mathcal{9}$:) together, each complete line of music is called a system. Notice below System 1 and System 2.

Now that you can play the treble notes/keys and the bass notes/buttons, it is time to practice these pieces with both hands. Follow these practice suggestions as you learn this new skill:

1. Play only the bass buttons ($\mathcal{9}$:) with your third and second fingers, pulling and pushing the bellows, out and in as marked. Notice at the end of System 2 you will continue pushing while playing G, then C.

2. "Shadow practice" both hands this way: (pressing keys and buttons with no sound).

   • Fasten the Bellows Straps

   • In measure 1, press the E on the right hand together with the C button on the left hand, holding the left hand C button while pressing the remaining E, then F, then G.

   • In measure 2, press the Gs on both hands and continue holding the left-hand G button while pressing F, then E, then D on the right-hand keys.

   • In measure 3, press both Cs and hold the left-hand C button while continuing to press the remaining C, and D, and E on the right-hand.

   • In measure 4, press the right-hand E together with the G button holding this G while pressing right-hand D then D. (Hold this second D a little longer.)

3. Continue to do this same style of shadow practicing for System 2.

4. Unfasten bellows straps and practice as you learned with #1 and #2 above, but pulling and pushing the bellows. Play Systems 1 and 2. Enjoy!

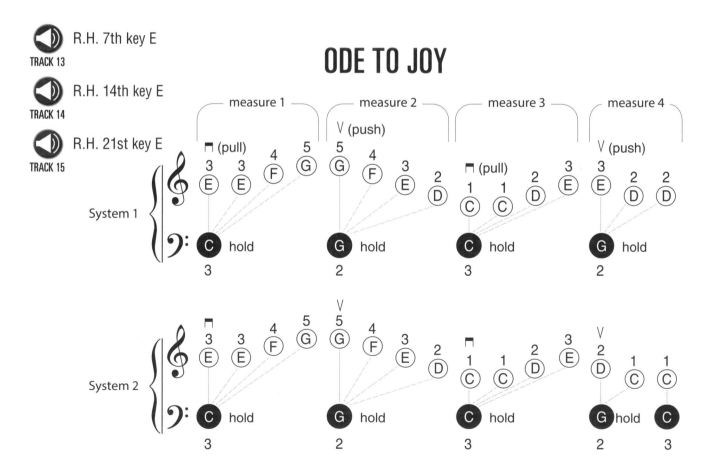

Continue to play with both hands, but move the right hand to different octaves.

TIME FOR ACTION WITH BOTH HANDS IN A NEW PLACE

Let's check out the left hand first: Locate the G button with your third finger (just above the C button moving up toward your head). Play while saying, "G" (pull bellows) and hold. Then, moving up (toward your head), locate the D button with your second finger. Play and say "D" (push). Move back down to the G button, play and say "G." Next, move back up to the D button, play and say "D." Repeat this several times.

You have played "Ode to Joy" with your right-hand third finger on the fourth key from your chin, the B key. Listen as you review this again (Track 7). As you play the right hand in that place while playing with both hands, it may remind you of a cello or baritone horn playing. That's okay, but you can hum or sing along more easily if you move your third finger to the next higher-sounding B key (the second B key on your keyboard—up one octave, or the eleventh key from your chin) and play there.

Play "Ode to Joy" with both hands several times, trying out each octave of the right hand. Decide which octave you like best; or perhaps you will like different octaves for different reasons.

ODE TO JOY

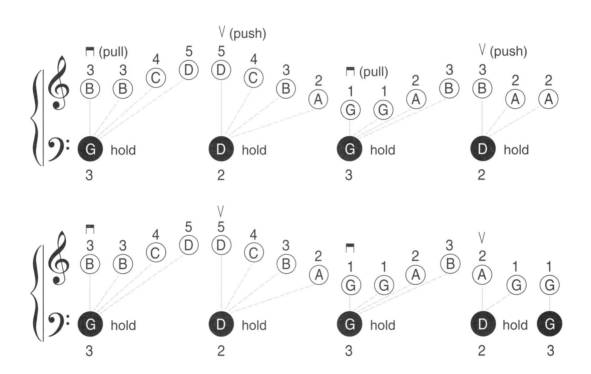

 R.H. finger 3 on 4th key from chin, B.

TRACK 16

 R.H. finger 3 on 11th key, B.

TRACK 17

 R.H. finger 3 on 18th key, B.

TRACK 18

LESSON 4

THE ACTION CONTINUES

To play "Mary Had a Little Lamb," it just so happens that we will again begin with our third finger on the E key. Arrange your other fingers as before: 1 – C, 2 – D, 3 – E, 4 – F, and 5 – G. In this familiar tune, you probably already know that some of the melody notes last longer than others. We will discuss counting very soon. For now, follow the timing you learned as a child. Here is a version for the right hand only. Learn this first.

TRACK 19

MARY HAD A LITTLE LAMB

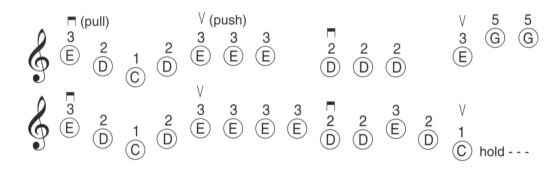

Follow the same practice suggestions you did when learning "Ode to Joy" with both hands: First, play bass buttons alone, pulling and pushing the bellows as indicated. Next, follow all "shadow practice" procedures (bellows fastened) for Systems 1 and 2, using both hands.

TRACK 20

Finally, with bellows unfastened, practice with both hands. When "Mary Had a Little Lamb" is going fairly well, play the right-hand melody one octave higher, and then two octaves higher.

MARY HAD A LITTLE LAMB

TRACK 21 R.H. finger 3 on 14th key, E.

TRACK 22 R.H. finger 3 on 21st key, E.

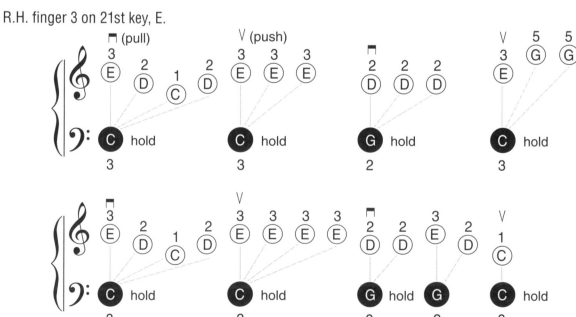

ACTION IN ANOTHER PLACE

Transposing "Mary Had a Little Lamb" will be as easy as transposing "Ode to Joy." Again, with your third finger, find the fourth key from your chin, the B key. Next, arrange your other fingers as before (1 – G, 2 – A, 3 – B, 4 – C, 5 – D). You are ready to try the song in another place! When you are reasonably proficient, and if you have opportunity to play while children sing, move the melody up one octave (or two octaves) and play it that way for singing. On pages 17 and 18, you will hear the given recording in the middle octave, while you play along in the first, second and third octaves.

TRACK 23

MARY HAD A LITTLE LAMB

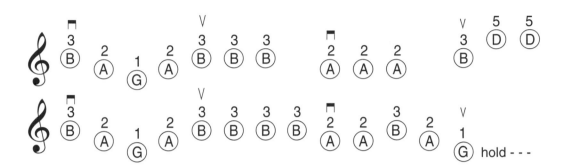

Locate the G button (just above the C button). Also, locate the D button (just above the G button). Study the left-hand part below and practice it first, pulling and pushing the bellows as marked. Next, "shadow practice" both hands with the bellows fastened as instructed before. Finally, unfasten the bellows and play normally with both hands. Then play again with the right hand one octave, then two octaves, higher.

TRACK 24

MARY HAD A LITTLE LAMB

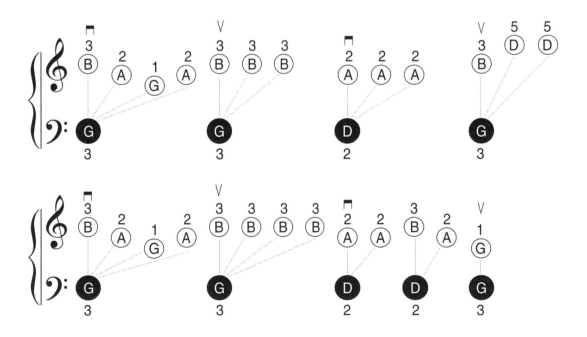

ACTION IN STILL ANOTHER PLACE

You have learned "Mary Had a Little Lamb" with both hands in several places and multiple octaves, so you are ready for an entirely new place.

This time, find the third key from your chin, the A key, with your tall/third finger. Arrange the other fingers side by side (F – 1, G – 2, A – 3, B – 4, C – 5). At this place, "Mary" will sound like a bass singer or even a tuba. Try it; but you may wish to move up an octave. If you do, also play it two octaves higher.

TRACK 25

MARY HAD A LITTLE LAMB

To prepare to play with both hands: First, turn back to "Bass Buttons Warm-ups" and review the third system of bass buttons that move from F to C. Practice this several times. Next, "shadow practice" with both hands, as on earlier pieces; then practice normally, using various octaves with the right hand. Be sure to pull and push as marked.

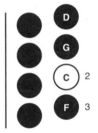

TRACK 26

MARY HAD A LITTLE LAMB

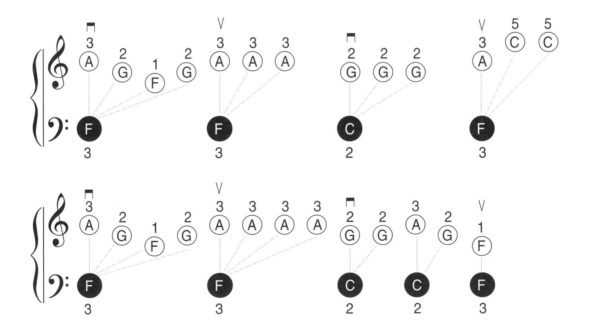

LESSON 5

PREPARING TO READ MUSIC

Note Values

Perhaps you noticed, as you played "Ode to Joy" and "Mary Had a Little Lamb," that certain notes were longer than others. Below is some information about how this works:

In nearly all music that has been composed during approximately the past four-hundred years, there is always (sometimes silent, but ever-present) an underlying, evenly-spaced pulse (dividing time evenly) in a repeated beat pattern for all notes that are played. (This underlying, evenly-spaced pulse is similar to using the constant measurements of inches – or feet, or yards – as an underlying, evenly-spaced unit of measurement when measuring a piece of furniture.)

So far, you have played mostly quarter notes. Quarter notes each receive one count (or beat, or pulse) and are played evenly; that is, they are and sound evenly spaced in time – just like inches are evenly spaced on a measuring stick. Study Illustration A.

Illustration A

TRACK 27

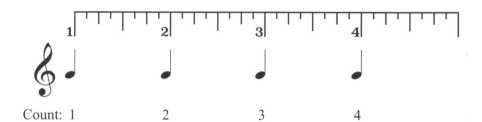

Then you played a few half notes. A half note receives two counts, and is held twice as long as a quarter note. Illustration B shows that a half note is held and sounds twice as long as a quarter note in time value, in exactly the same way that two inches is twice as long as one inch in a spatial relationship. (If a quarter note lasts one second, a half note lasts two seconds.)

Illustration B

TRACK 28

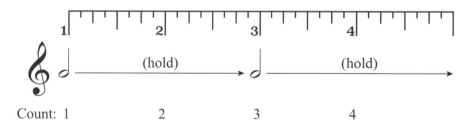

Also, you have played whole notes. A whole note lasts four counts. Notice in Illustration C that a whole note would be held for the same amount of time it would take to play four quarter notes or two half notes. If a quarter note lasts one second, a whole note lasts four seconds.)

Illustration C

TRACK 29

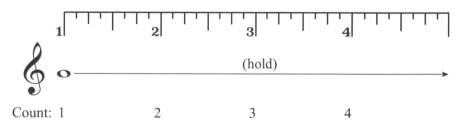

This would be an excellent time to review pages 8 through 18. Play three or four pages each day, and then do it again.

As you have played with both hands, you have played the combinations shown below. Tap the top notes with your right hand; tap the bottom notes with your left hand.

Illustration D

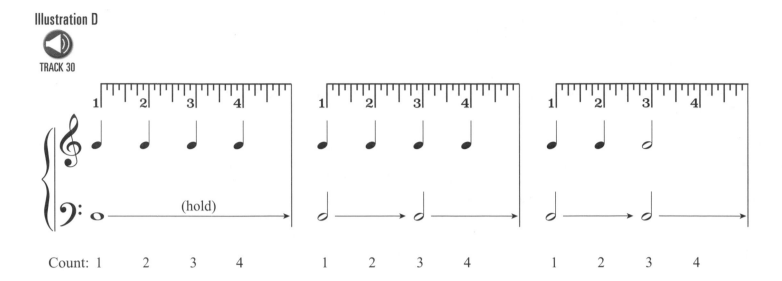

The Grand Staff

Accordion music is written on the grand staff, using the treble clef for the right hand and the bass clef for the left hand. (Review page 6, "The Grand Staff.") Each clef has five lines and four spaces. Notes written on the spaces are between the lines. When notes are written on the lines, the line actually intersects the notehead.

Time Signatures

After the clef signs, there is a time signature (meter signature). We will study 4/4 meter first. The 4 on the top means that every measure receives four counts, followed by a bar line. Bar lines appear throughout a piece, creating measures. (We will discuss the 4 on the bottom later.)

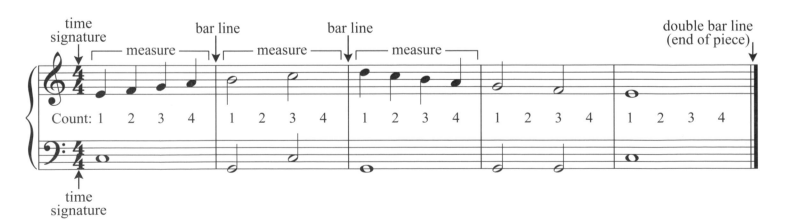

BEGINNING TO READ MUSIC FOR REAL

Using the grand staff, on this and the following few pages you will see the music notation for "Ode to Joy" and "Mary Had a Little Lamb" in several of the places where you have already played them. On System 1, you will see letters inside the noteheads, then on System 2, notation without letters. Learn to recognize the notes by their positions on the lines or spaces. If you wish, you can review the pieces on the earlier pages, but you should begin to focus on learning to read real notation.

Can you find the quarter notes that receive one count? There are quite a few. Can you also locate a few half notes? Remember, each half note receives two counts. (Say, "half – note" or "two – counts."*) Then you can see quite a few whole notes, especially on the bass-clef part. These four-count notes are held while you play four quarter notes with the other hand (or two quarters and a half note).

TRACK 31

ODE TO JOY

By Ludwig van Beethoven

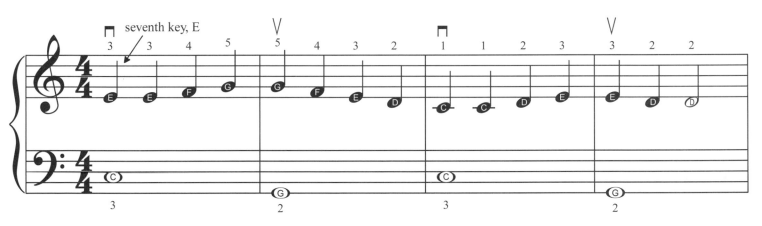

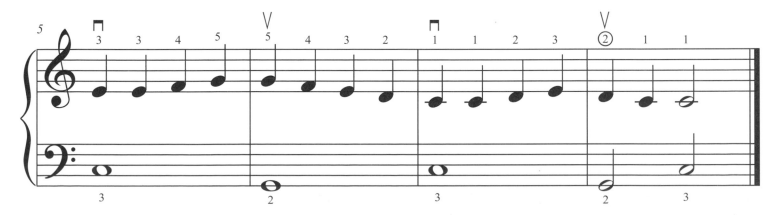

You will use both the third and the second fingers for the bass part for each of these pieces, so locate the two bass buttons in the fundamental row. They will be beside each other for these early pieces. For now, you will often be aided by having the letter names appear inside the noteheads. However, study the notes so you can become a real reader when this help is no longer available. Check out pieces in other music books, and see how many notes (without helps) you can identify as you compare them to the notes you are learning in this method.

* From *Piano ABC's Level One*, p. 9, used by permission.

ODE TO JOY

By Ludwig van Beethoven

MARY HAD A LITTLE LAMB

Traditional

Study the treble notes below: These are notes you have read in "Ode to Joy" and "Mary Had a Little Lamb."

Study the bass notes below: These are notes you are currently using.

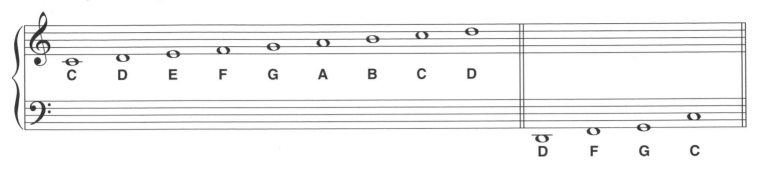

MARY HAD A LITTLE LAMB

TRACK 34

Traditional

PREPARING TO READ THE BASS CLEF

You have played these four bass notes so far. Learn to identify them:

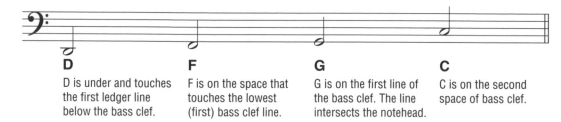

D
D is under and touches the first ledger line below the bass clef.

F
F is on the space that touches the lowest (first) bass clef line.

G
G is on the first line of the bass clef. The line intersects the notehead.

C
C is on the second space of bass clef.

Since the single bass notes are written on just seven lines and spaces, you have only three more notes (E, A, and B) to learn to recognize and read. You will soon learn a few flats and sharps (like B♭ and F♯), but the lines and spaces used for these notes are the same and are always in alphabetical order starting with D (D E F G A B C).

Study these seven bass notes and locate F, C, G, and D.

D   E   F   G   A   B   C

Now, thinking alphabetically, fill in the blanks to name all the bass clef notes.

D   __   __   G   __   __   C

Below are the single bass notes written on the spaces, followed by the bass notes written on lines. Memorize these little mnemonic tricks so you can easily remember how to read these notes.

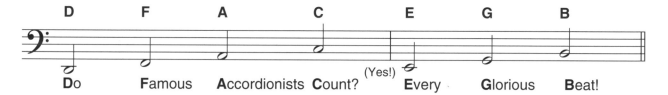

Do   **F**amous   **A**ccordionists   **C**ount?   (Yes!) **E**very   **G**lorious   **B**eat!

See how well you can recognize these bass notes by reading alphabetically in sets of three notes. Fill in the missing letter names for the notes below:

A   _   C   F   _   A   D   _   F   G   _   B   E   _   G

LESSON 6
LEARNING TO CONDUCT 4/4 METER*

Learning to conduct will help you keep a steady beat as you learn how to count. Keeping a steady beat is as important to playing music correctly as a ruler or yardstick (meter stick) is for measuring materials correctly for sewing or woodworking.

Study the illustration below to learn how to conduct in 4/4 meter. Follow the arrows, counting aloud evenly and steadily, and feel a strong pulse on each count. Each conducting movement equals one count. Count aloud: "1-2-3-4."

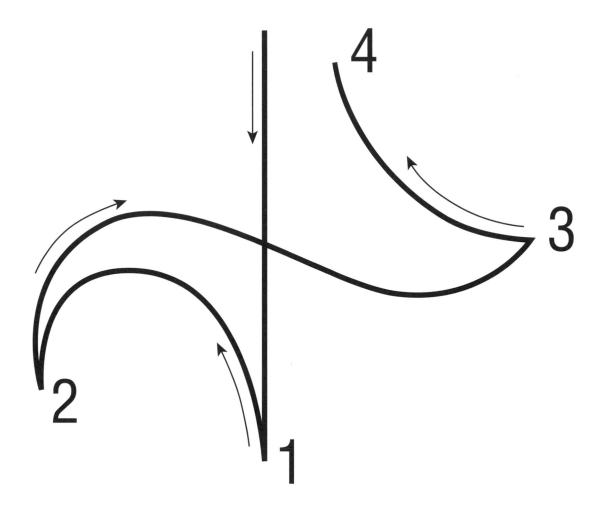

4/4 meter means there are four counts in each measure. As we saw on page 20, a measure is the space between the bar lines.

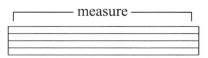

The bottom 4 reminds us that the quarter (1/4) note receives one count. The quarter note (♩) is 1/4 of a whole note.

* Adapted from *Piano ABC's Level One* and Patent No. US 7,453,036 B1, used by permission.

RHYTHM*

Rhythm involves playing notes, one after another, that are held for a short time, a long time, or a longer time. Counting steadily is absolutely necessary to play rhythm correctly. Conducting while counting will help you understand rhythm. Below we will learn about short notes, long notes, and longer notes—and how to count and tap them rhythmically over a steady beat.

TRACK 35

This is a quarter note: ♩
It gets one count.
Tap it and say "one" and lift your hand immediately.

Here are two quarter notes: ♩ ♩
Tap each one saying "one" "one" as you tap.
Tap and lift your hand immediately.

♩
one

♩ ♩
one   one

Now let's tap steadily the following quarter notes. Say the little chant below the notes and tap a quarter note with each syllable or word. Be-sure-you-speak-like-a-ro-bot.

quar - ter   note,   tap   each   note   one   count

TRACK 36

This is a half note: ♩
It gets two counts.

Below are four half notes.
Tap and hold each half note as
you say "half note" or "two counts."

♩ ——(hold)——→
two   counts

speak-e-ven-ly-like-a-ro-bot.

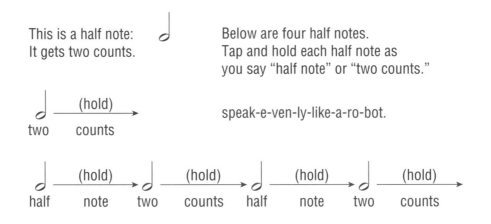

♩ ——(hold)——→ ♩ ——(hold)——→ ♩ ——(hold)——→ ♩ ——(hold)——→
half   note   two   counts   half   note   two   counts

TRACK 37

This is a whole note: 𝅝
It gets four counts.
Tap and hold it all the time as you say:

𝅝 ————(hold)————→
whole   note   four   counts

𝅝 ————(hold)————→ 𝅝 ————(hold)————→
whole   note   four   counts   one   two   three   four

---

* Concepts and graphics adapted from *Piano ABC's Level One* and Patent No. US 7,453,036 B1, used by permission.

COUNTING HELPS RHYTHM MAKE SENSE

If you should have a metronome, set it at 60 beats per minute. Each beat you hear equals a quarter (♩). Tap and count "1-2-3-4" – one tap = one beat. You have just counted and tapped four quarter notes. Each beat lasts one second. Next, tap with the first beat and *hold* for the next beat as you say "1-2." Now you have counted and tapped a half note (♩). The half note lasts two counts or two seconds. Remember, every count is spaced evenly during the passage of time, just like the inches on a ruler are spaced evenly as you measure cloth, wood, or any object. Compare what you are learning about quarter notes, half notes, and whole notes to the measurements of a ruler, as illustrated.

The first example, illustrated with the ruler measurement, can be tapped with either hand. The others are tapped with both hands (right hand 𝄞, left hand 𝄢). Sometimes the hands will tap the same rhythm; but other times, one will hold a half note for two counts while the other taps two quarter notes, or one will hold a whole note four counts while the other hand taps quarter notes or half notes or various combinations. Practice this page with metronome settings at 72, 84, and 100.

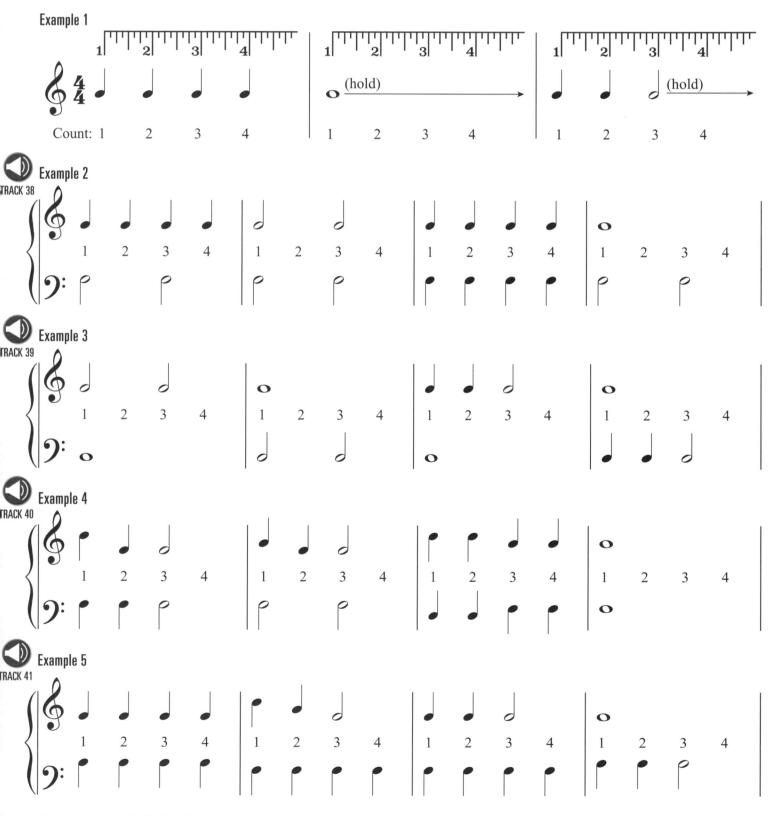

Review pages 19-27. Reviewing three pages a day, do it twice.

Notes to study for "Three Jolly Fishermen"

THREE JOLLY FISHERMEN

Traditional

TRACK 42

LESSON 7
MORE ABOUT NOTE READING: TREBLE AND BASS

The treble clef is also called the G clef. This clef sign* derived from the letter G, as shown below:

The French word "clef" means "key" and so it is. As a key lets you into a house so you can move around to any room, so, when you find the G line from the clef, you can name any other note by moving up or down alphabetically.

Remember, notes are written on lines and spaces. Review these alphabetical notes in sets of seven. Notice that the first A, B, and C are on lines and spaces below the clef. These are called *ledger lines and spaces* and follow the same alphabetical/line-space procedures as all the other notes. Review these notes on page 7, "The Treble Keyboard."

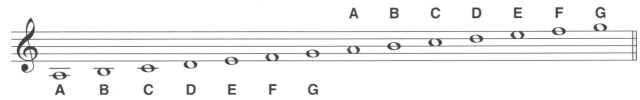

Below are some tricks to help you read line and space treble-clef notes more quickly.

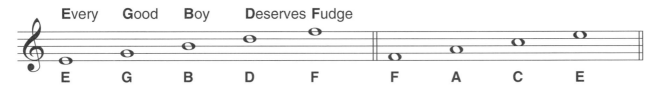

The bass clef is also called the F clef. The bass clef sign** derived from the letter F, as shown below:

Find the F line from the clef; then you can name any other note by moving up or down alphabetically.

Review the single bass notes you studied on page 24, "Preparing to Read the Bass Clef," and remember that the stems go up. Study the notes below for the chords and notice that the stems go down. When you play the chords indicated by these notes, you will hear three tones at once.

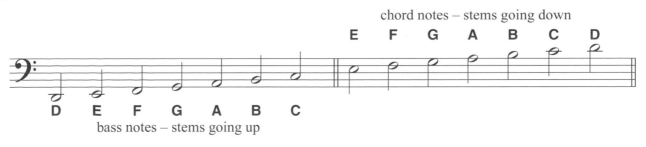

* *Harvard Dictionary of Music* and Wikipedia

** mrgriffithstrings.weebly.com

THE BASS BUTTONS

The bass buttons add accompaniment – as harmony, rhythm, counter-melodies, and other interesting patterns – to the melody (which is usually – but not always – played by the right hand on the treble keyboard). You have already played single bass tones with the melody. Now we will add major chords, which are found in the third row from the bellows, as illustrated below.

Finger numbers were learned at the same time you learned the finger numbers for the right hand, and they are the same: thumbs – one, pointer – two, tall man – three, ring man – four, and pinkie – five. You will use fingers 2, 3, 4, and 5 to play the bass buttons.

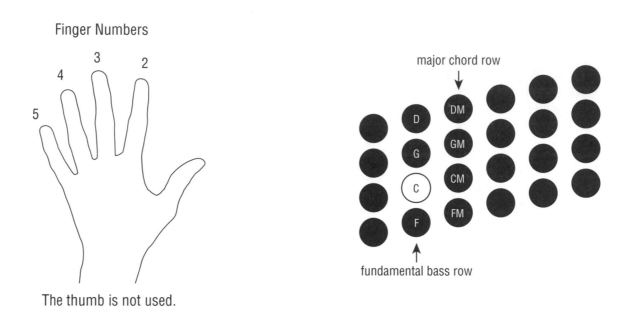

The thumb is not used.

With your third (3) finger, play the C button. Keep the third finger on the C button and find the C major chord with your second finger. Play this C major chord button and listen to the sound of three tones sounding together. Now, play the C bass button and C major chord button together with your third and second fingers.

Single bass notes and major chord notes are written below in the seven measures of bass clef music. Study the notes and patterns in measures 1 and 2 and play this C bass and C major chord, both separately and together. Next, study the G bass and G major chord in measures 3 and 4 and play this. Finally, practice moving back and forth from C and C major to G and G major several times, as notated. Notice the repeat sign, which means to repeat all seven measures. In this case, you may repeat as many times as you like.

TRACK 43

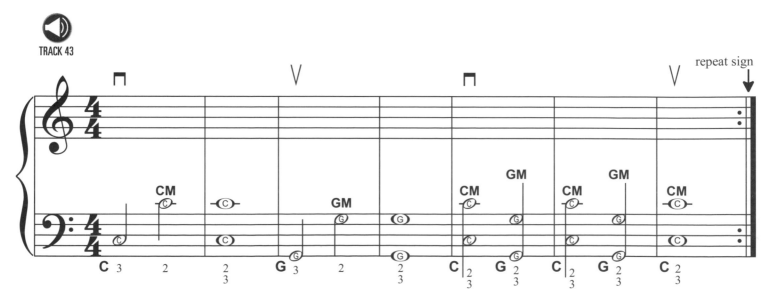

Left-hand fingers 3 and 2 will play C and C major and G and G major on systems 1 and 3. Arrange fingers 4, 3, 2 on F, C, and G for system 2.

Study the treble (right hand) notes below. Notice that you will play in two places with the right hand.

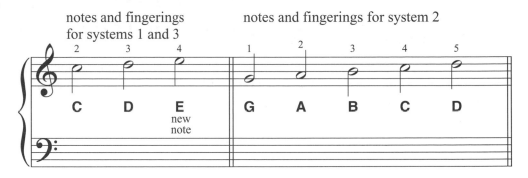

notes and fingerings for systems 1 and 3

notes and fingerings for system 2

AU CLAIR DE LA LUNE

French Folksong

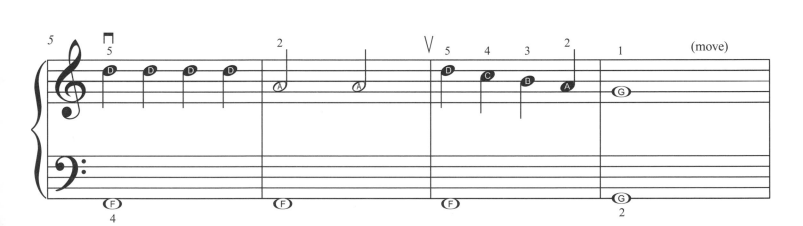

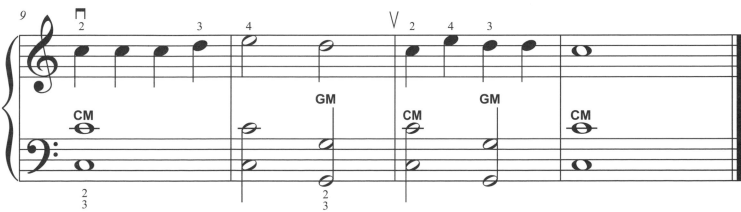

LESSON 8
CHORD SYMBOLS AND WARM-UPS FOR "LIGHTLY ROW"

Beginning with your next pieces and continuing throughout this book, you will see capital letters like G, C, D, F, etc. just above the grand staff. These are chord symbols for the left hand. Chord symbols are frequently used to let musicians know the harmonies that accompany the melody.

Below are a few warm-ups for your next piece, "Lightly Row," and some practice suggestions. Learning to practice effectively will make learning to play much more efficient and enjoyable.

Read chord symbols (capital letters) and M for major chords. Learn this well. It will help with the next warm-up.

TRACK 45

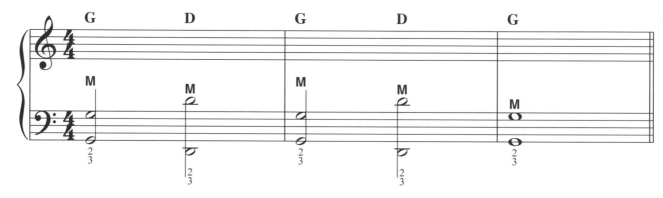

Notice the new notation system in which letters are left of the notehead, rather than inside. Practice measure 1 several times diligently, and you will be more successful with measure 2. Then, practice measure 3 several times, and measure 4 will seem fairly easy. If you pull bellows out for measure 1, you may repeat it pushing in. You may do this for each measure as many times as you repeat it.

TRACK 46

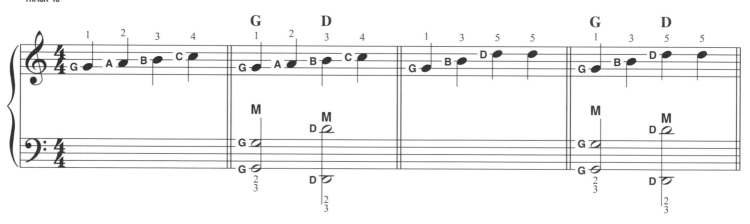

TRACK 47 Use a bouncy touch to play all quarter notes; then, hold the half note two counts. In the first two measures, think "Chimp, chimp, chaw – aw." In the past, students have been taught to lift each finger before playing a button. This produces tension and is unnecessary. Let fingers remain on buttons (touching) and press down using a gentle, bouncy technique. In each example below, listen to the track; then, practice as directed before playing with the track.

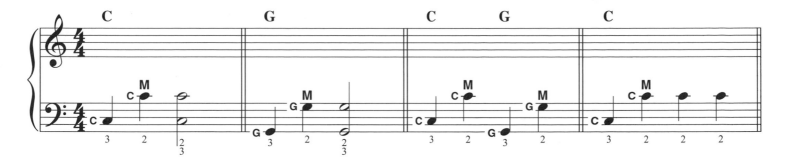

TRACK 48 Practice measure 1 several times; when ready, learn measure 2. Follow the same strategy for measures 3 and 4. Remember to use a bouncy technique when playing bass-chord patterns with the left hand.

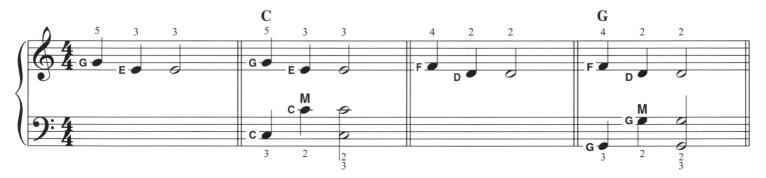

TRACK 49 Each hand is rather busy in the next warm-up. Begin slower than you think you should. Be sure to repeat measure 1 until it is easy. Do the same with measure 2. Then, again, slow down a bit and play with both hands until it's easy.

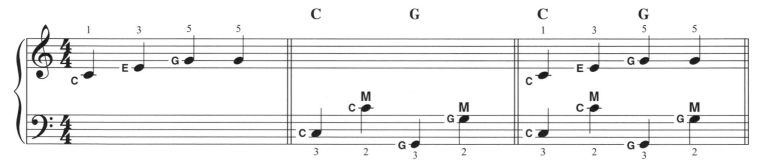

TRACK 50 Learn measure 1 (fairly easy), then practice measure 2 (also fairly easy); then play both hands together. Have fun!

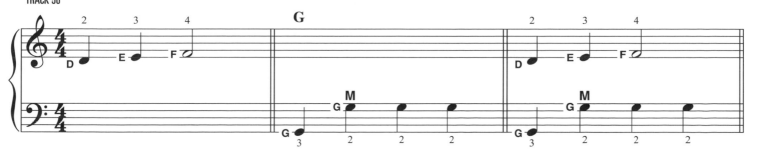

33

Study and learn to read the notes for "Lightly Row:"

Measures 1-16

Measures 17-36

RESTS ARE SIGNS OF SILENCE

whole rest

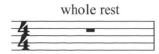

A whole rest is a small rectangle that hangs from the fourth line on the clef. It means to be silent for four counts. You will see whole rests on the next page in measures 17 and 18 on the treble clef, because only the left hand plays during these two measures.

LIGHTLY ROW

TRACK 51

Traditional Folksong

(move from 1 to 5 on G)

LESSON 9

QUARTER REST

A quarter rest (𝄽) is a sign of silence that receives one count, just like its counterpart the quarter note.

Count: 1   2   3   4

WARM-UPS FOR "HAPPY BLUES"

Practice the right-hand part (measure 1) of "Happy Blues" a few times, counting "1-2-3-4." Next, practice the left-hand (measure 2) a few more times, counting "1-2-3-4." Then, play both hands together until it is easy.

TRACK 52

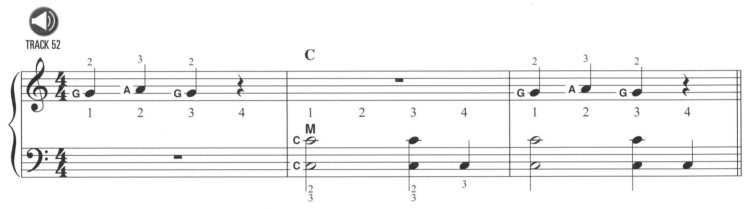

We will learn the trickiest part of "Happy Blues" next. In the following warm-up, you will need to play the bass buttons in three different places. Study the bass button and fingering illustrations below; practice until you can readily locate these various places.

The seventh chord row is next to the last row of buttons before the wrist strap.

First, locate C and C major; play with 3 and 2. Next, find F and F seventh and play with 4 and 2. Finally, find G and G seventh and play with 3 and 2.

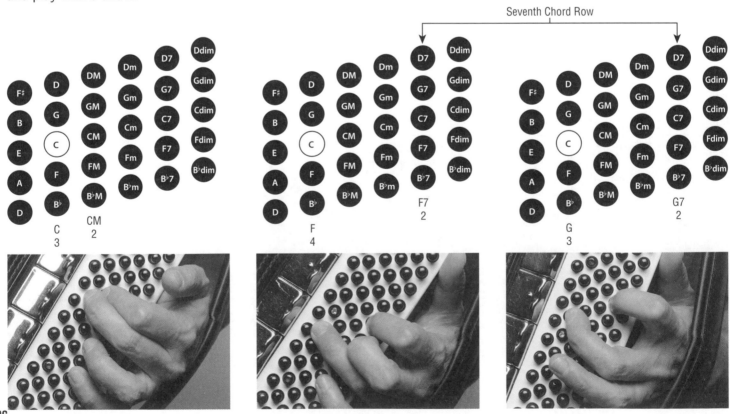

36

TRACK 53
Careful attention, diligence, and cheerful patience will yield success on this bass pattern.

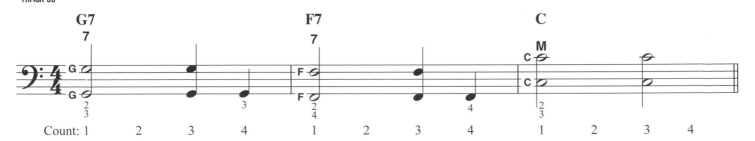

TRACK 54
The treble part is a bit easier. Just remember to move to the new starting note in each measure with your second finger.

TRACK 55
When you feel ready, try this with both hands. Practice first in your head, mentally rehearsing the move of hands at each measure. When that makes sense, try it for real. You can do this!

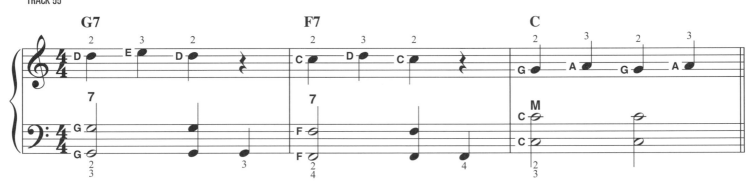

Below is the basic pattern for any 12-bar blues, with one chord/harmony per bar (measure):

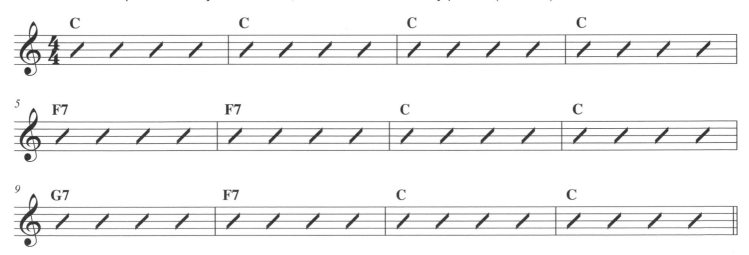

As you are becoming familiar with seventh chords on pages 36 and 37, take several days to review pages 28-31 and 32-35. Also, pick out three old pieces to play every day for enjoyment.

Treble notes to study for "Happy Blues"

G   A   (B)   C   D   E

HAPPY BLUES

TRACK 56

Traditional

LESSON 10
LEARNING TO CONDUCT 3/4 METER*

Below is the conducting pattern for the 3/4 time signature. Learn to conduct and count this new pattern:

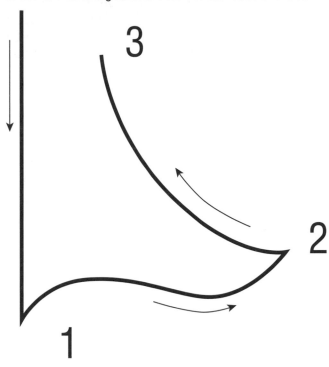

A dotted half note receives 3 counts. The half note receives two counts and the dot adds one more count:

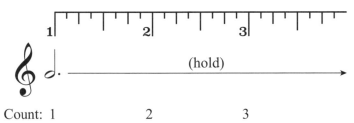

Notice the new graphics that give a visual representation of the note values:

One circle represents one quarter note ♩, tap one count.

Two circles represent a half note, two counts ♩, tap the first circle and hold for the other circle.

Three circles joined together mean a dotted half note, three counts ♩., tap the first circle and hold for the other circles.

Next, study, count, and tap the rhythmic practice example.

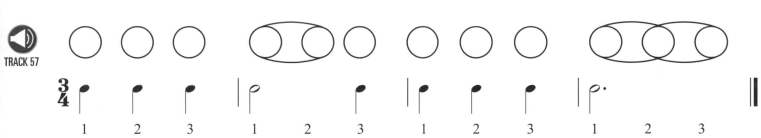

TRACK 57

* Adapted from *Piano ABC's Level One* and Patent No. US 7,453,036 B1, used by permission.

MOVING AROUND THE KEYBOARD – Extensions

There are several ways to move around the treble keyboard with your right hand. We have already learned to simply move your whole hand from one place to another (e.g., the Treble Keyboard page, several examples of "Ode to Joy" and "Mary Had a Little Lamb," "Lightly Row," "Happy Blues," and other pieces). On this page, we will learn several extensions.

Before we begin the exercises below: Open your hand, like a yawn. Notice how far apart from each other you can extend your fingers. Now, open as wide as possible the thumb to the second finger, then open wide the second and third finger, third and fourth, and fourth and fifth. The varied distances are normal. As you play the keyboard of your accordion, you will learn to play many pieces in which extensions between any or all fingers will be necessary.

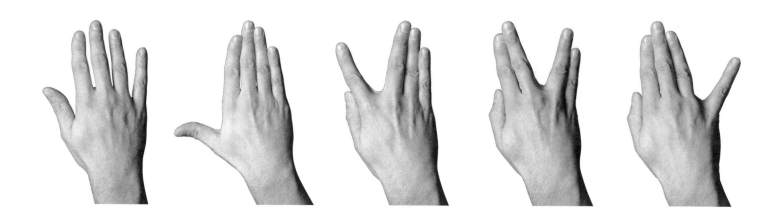

In Extension 1, the thumb plays D after E, then extends down to play C after E.

In Extension 2, the thumb begins playing F, then later extends down to E, which creates another extension when the second finger remains on G.

Extension 1

Extension 2

Extension 1 will be used first in "Blow the Man Down." But don't be surprised if you see similar extensions in later pieces.

These extensions from four to one and one to two are common, and you will find many extensions of the thumb as you learn other pieces in the book. Thumb extensions are easy because the thumb can extend farther than any other finger.

In Extension 3, notice that finger 5 will probably rest on G as you begin this exercise. Extend it up to A taking fingers 4 and 3 along, but leave the thumb on C. Notice that you will return finger 4 to F, exactly where you started the exercise.

Extension 3

MOVING AROUND THE BUTTONS – Alternate Basses and Counterbasses

From this point forward, as you play the fundamental bass with any of its chords (C with C major, G with G major or G seventh), the music will often include the alternate bass and sometimes the counterbass. The alternate bass is in every case the bass just above the fundamental bass. (Think vertically, from floor to ceiling.) The alternate for F is C, the alternate for C is G, the alternate for G is D, and so forth.

The counterbass button is near the bellows and slightly down toward the floor. A is the counterbass for F; E is the counterbass for C; B is the counterbass for G; and so forth. (See bass/chord chart on page 80). Notes for counterbasses are identified by a straight line underneath that note.

Locate the fundamental basses with their nearby alternating basses and counterbasses. Note the two possible fingerings. Try both fingerings in the examples.

TRACK 58

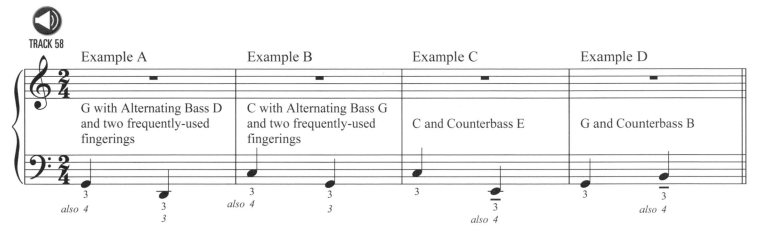

Now, play these very typical bass/chord patterns using fundamental, alternating, and counterbasses.

TRACK 59

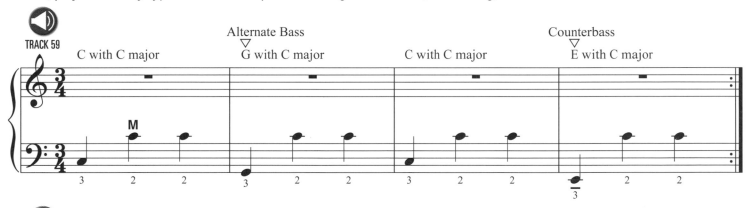

TRACK 60

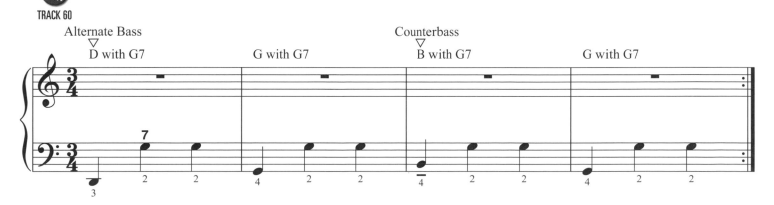

Can you name these single bass notes and chord names? (Answers below)

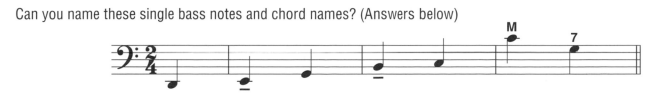

Answers: D, E (Counterbass of C), G, B (Counterbass of G), C, C Major, G Seventh

Read the notes below.

Listen to the track; but before you play with the track, practice:
System 1 – eight times, System 2 – twelve times,
System 3 – twelve times, System 4 – eight times.

TRACK 61

BLOW THE MAN DOWN

Traditional Sea Chantey

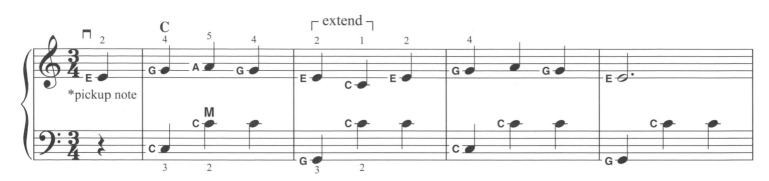

*pickup note

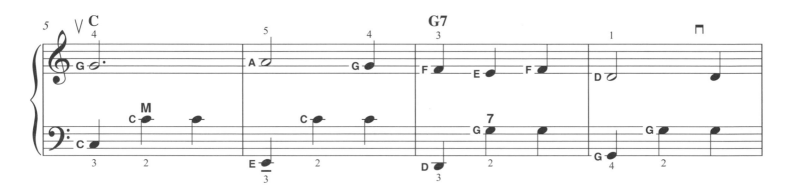

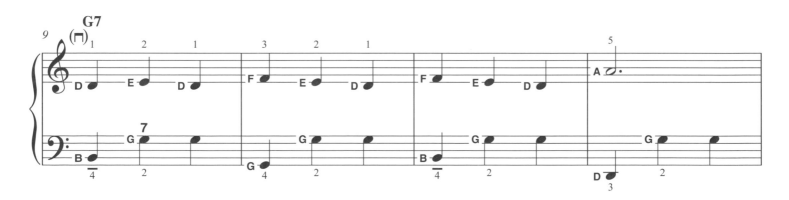

*Pickup notes: When a piece begins on a beat other than beat 1, you have an incomplete measure. The "missing" beats are found in the last measure. Begin by counting "1–2" and start playing on count "3."

LESSON 11

NOTE-READING PRACTICE

Note-reading proficiency makes learning music easier. You already know that notes proceed in alphabetical order, alternating on lines and spaces.

Two complete sets of seven alphabetical notes in the treble clef are illustrated in the first clef of music below. Study them and then fill in the blanks. Notice that the first three notes, which are below the treble clef (A, B, C), are on ledger lines and a space below a ledger line (short lines that extend note writing above or below the five-line clef). Yet, they still proceed in alternating line-space-line order just like all other notes.

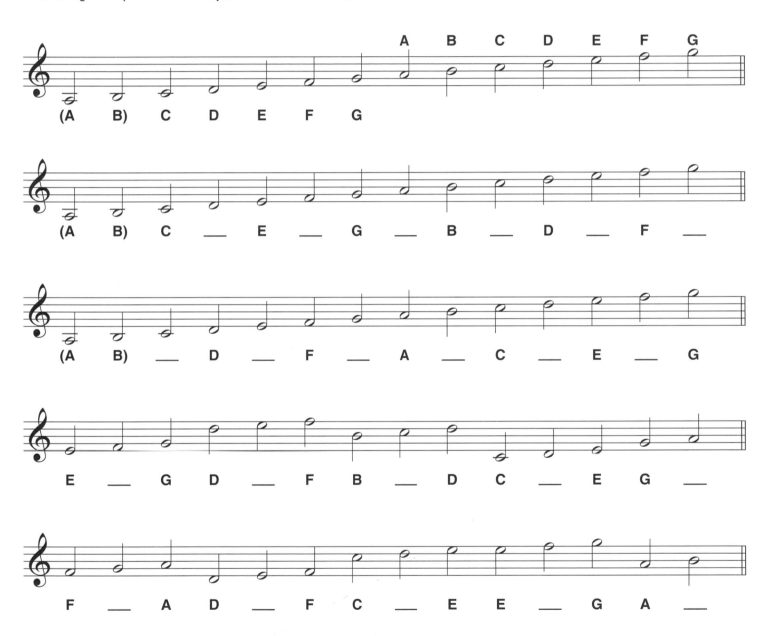

Between pages 38 and 43, there are several important concepts to review. Study these again. Also, you will find it wise to practice "Blow the Man Down" six times for every two times you practice "Happy Blues."

KEY SIGNATURES AND FLATS

A flat sign (♭) or a sharp (#) sign placed at the beginning of a piece becomes a key signature. When there is a B♭ in the key signature, this sign automatically turns all notes that look like B into B♭s. Remembering always to flat or sharp whatever is in the key signature is an important skill to tuck into your alert brain.

The next piece you will learn is in the key of F major and has one flat, B♭, which appears in both the treble and bass clefs. There are three B♭s on your keyboard. Find them all and play them. B♭ is the black key immediately before the B key and nearer to your chin.

Key of F major
one flat, B♭

Notice that the third line intersects the "roundish" section of the B♭ sign in the key signature, in the same way that the third line intersects the notehead of the note, B♭.

B♭   B♭

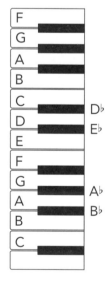

Can you find the D♭, A♭, E♭, and B♭ below on your keyboard? The B♭ note doesn't need another flat in front of it because it is already flatted by the key signature.

D♭   A♭   E♭   B♭

Remember the flat key is the black key immediately next to the letter name key and nearer to your chin.

A natural sign (♮) cancels a flat.

COUNTERBASS, FUNDAMENTAL BASS, AND MAJOR CHORD ROWS

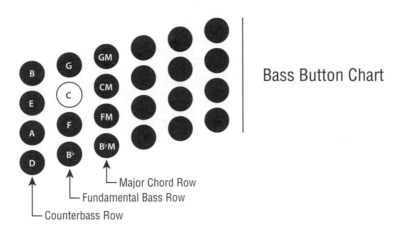

Bass Button Chart

Major Chord Row
Fundamental Bass Row
Counterbass Row

Bass patterns: Beginning with your second finger, play the fundamental bass button C. Next, with your third finger, play F. Then, play B♭ with your fourth finger. Now, find the D counterbass of B♭, and play with your fourth finger. Finally, in the fourth measure, play the bass solo pattern that uses the second finger on C and the fourth finger on the D counterbass.

TRACK 62

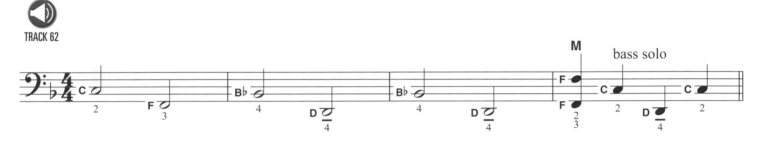

Now practice this bass pattern from the traditional folksong "Marianne."

TRACK 63

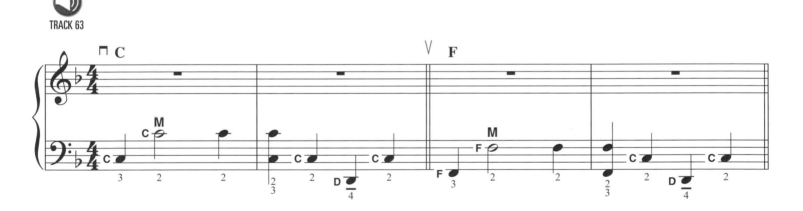

Ties: Ties make it possible for notes to last as long as you like. For example, what happens if you want a note to last six counts and there are only two counts left in the measure? Using a tie, connect it to the same note in the next measure. Add the values of the tied notes to find out how many counts the note lasts.

TRACK 64

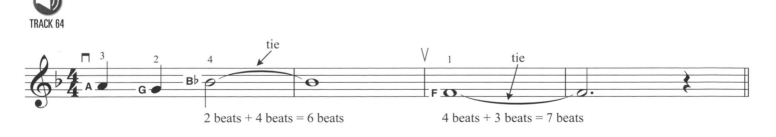

2 beats + 4 beats = 6 beats   4 beats + 3 beats = 7 beats

Study these notes as you prepare to learn "Marianne."

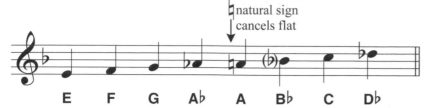

natural sign
cancels flat

E F G A♭ A B♭ C D♭

There are two accidentals in the introduction of "Marianne," D♭ and A♭. Accidentals apply only to the measure in which they appear.

MARIANNE

TRACK 65

Traditional

LESSON 12

EIGHTH NOTES*

Eighth notes often appear in pairs or sets of four notes, as illustrated below. They look similar to quarter notes, with one important difference: They are joined with a beam that identifies them as eighth notes. Eighth notes move twice as fast as quarter notes.

Below is a helpful visual approach that associates graphic drawings with note values. Study these and think about how they show the differences between long, short, and shorter notes.

◯ A circle represents a quarter note (one circle, one count).

⬭ Two circles joined together relate to a half note. (Tap once, hold two counts).

◖◗ Half circles stand for eighth notes, each eighth note getting half a count. Two eighth notes equal one quarter note in time value.

Observe how these graphics reflect the various note values:

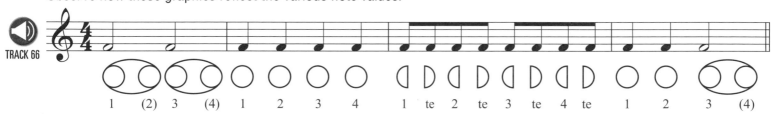

Count and tap this rhythmic example. Tap and hold half notes for two counts, tap quarter notes once each, tap twice per beat (count) for eighth notes.

Try this another way, using words rather than number counting.

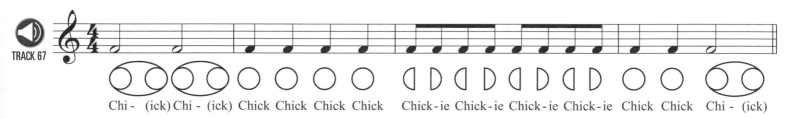

Following is a rhythmic warm-up for the introduction of "Old MacDonald." Practice counting, tapping, and/or using words as you did above.

---

* Adapted from *Piano ABC's Level One* and Patent No. US 7,453,036 B1, used by permission.

Practice this bass pattern at least a dozen times; it appears several times in "Old MacDonald." Notice the use of counterbasses A (above F), E (above C), and B♭, which is still fairly new.

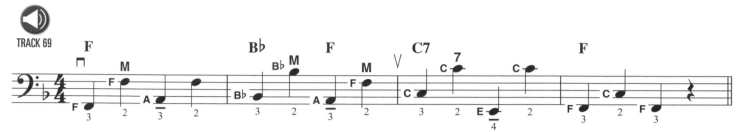

Notes for "Old MacDonald."

half rest

A half rest sits on the third line. It means to be silent for two counts. Notice several in measures 13, 15, and 16.

OLD MacDONALD HAD A FARM

Traditional

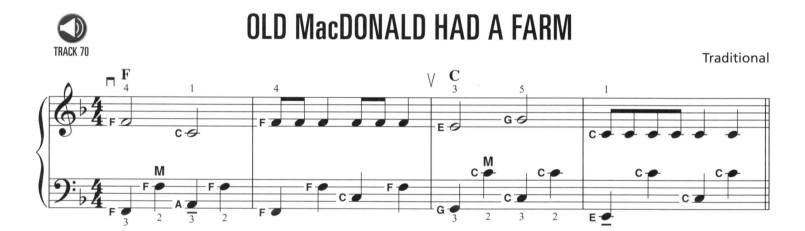

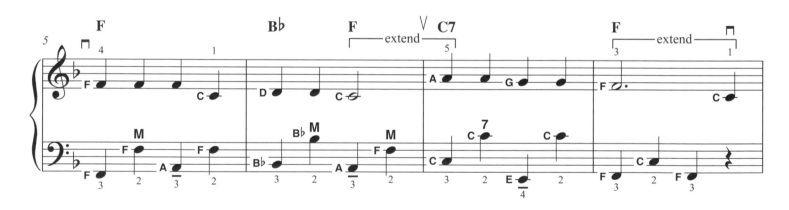

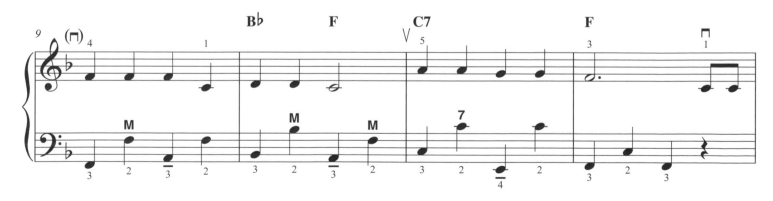

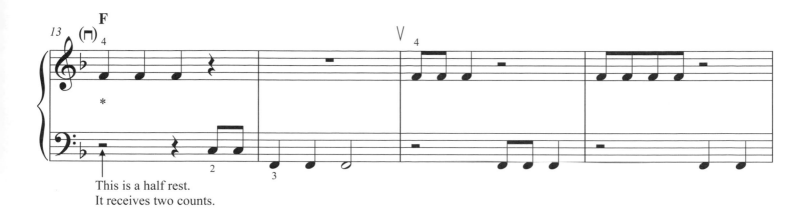

This is a half rest.
It receives two counts.

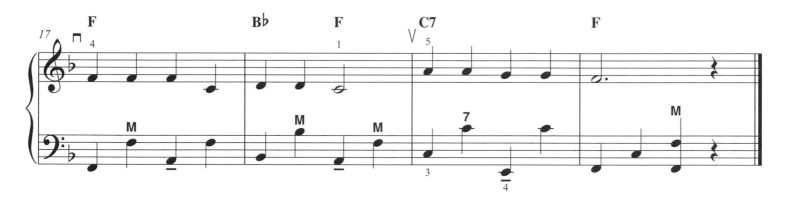

*Measures 13-16 can later be repeated as necessary for cows with "moos," ducks with "quacks," pigs with "oinks," etc.

A right-hand crossover is another way to move around the keyboard. It is easy to cross a finger over a thumb. With your hand shaped around an imaginary bubble and with very gently rounded finger joints, allow the finger to step with agility over the standing thumb. This technique will appear increasingly as one of the most-often-used ways of getting around the keyboard.

TRACK 71   TRACK 72

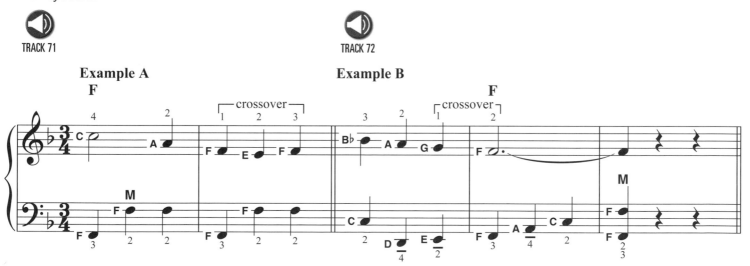

** Study the bass button chart a few pages back as you learn the left-hand notes and buttons in the examples above.

For the next week or two (or more if you like) review pages 44-49. Then review pages 24-38 and add three tunes to your daily review "practice/play" for fun. Finally, review pages 39-49.

Notes for this piece

C (D) E F G A Bb C D

After first listening to the track, do yourself a favor and practice each system eight to twelve times even for several days before playing with the track.

OH WHERE, OH WHERE HAS MY LITTLE DOG GONE

Traditional

TRACK 73

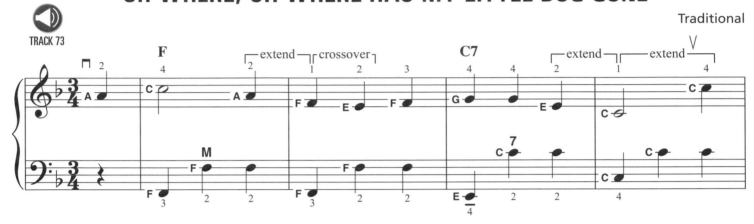

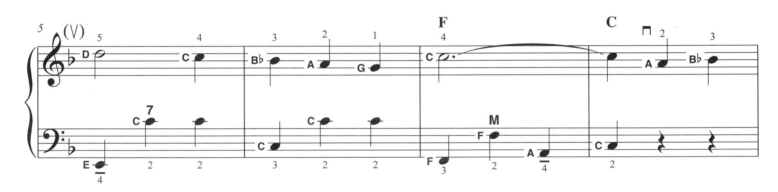

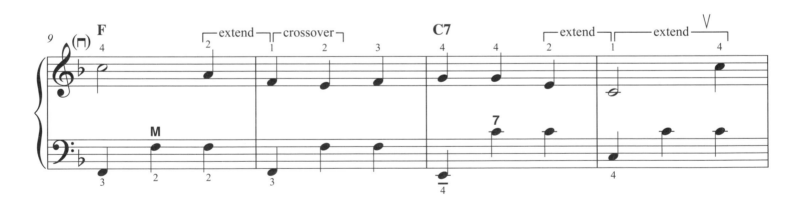

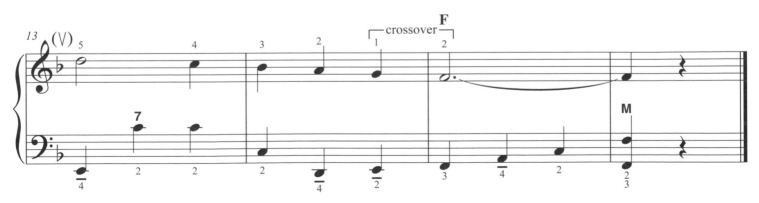

LESSON 13

RHYTHMIC PREPARATION* FOR "DU, DU LIEGST MIR IM HERZEN"

Study the rhythmic examples below. Compare the second measures of both examples. Be alert and ready to play the "1 te" rhythm in the second measure of the second example.

Count while tapping the 𝄞 part with your right hand. Then, count while tapping the 𝄢 part with your left hand. Next, count and tap both hands at the same time for each example.

Finally, play both examples with both hands until they are easy.

Open the bellows approximately six inches.

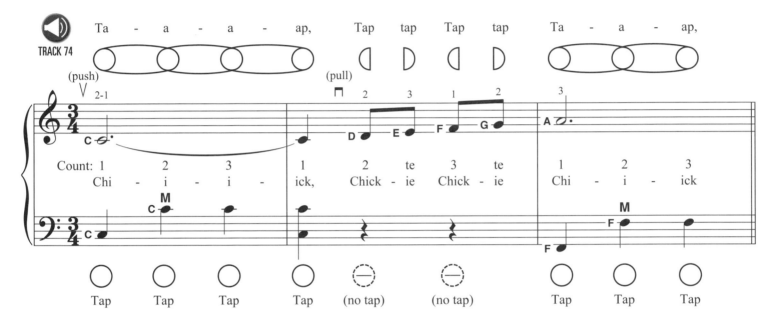

Open the bellows approximately six inches.

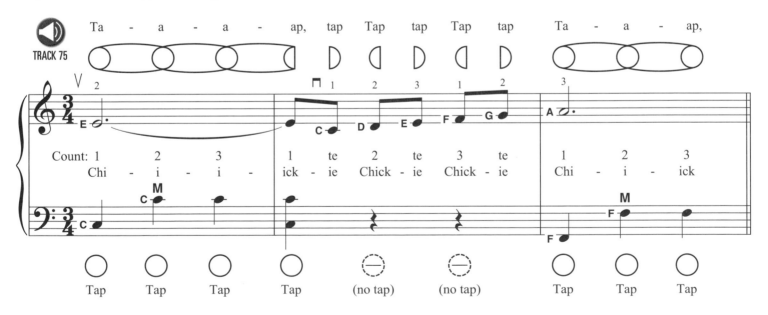

Your next pieces, "Du, du liegst mir im Herzen" and "Maori Farewell Song," on pages 56 and 57, both have first and second endings. The first endings have repeat signs. The easy explanation for first and second endings is this: the first ending is played only the first time, but not the second time; whereas, the second ending is played the second (repeat) time only, and is not played the first time.

* Adapted from *Piano ABC's Level One* and Patent No. US 7,453,036 B1, used by permission.

51

Notes to know for this song:

B C D E F F♯ G A B C

F♯ (F-sharp) is the black key immediately after the white key F as you move toward your knee.

Key for new note
F♯ (measure 32)

TRACK 76

DU, DU LIEGST MIR IM HERZEN

German Folksong

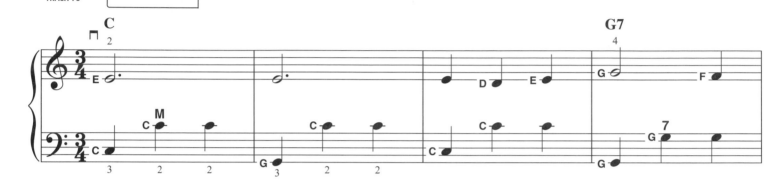

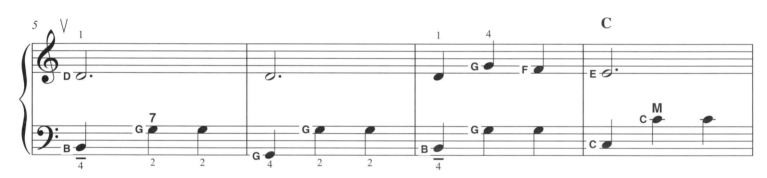

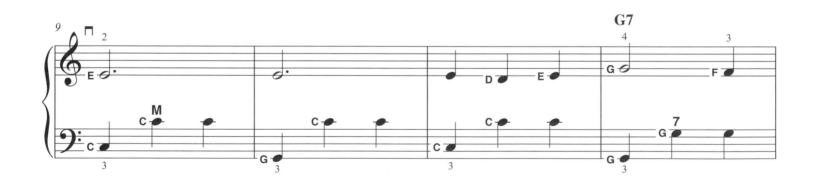

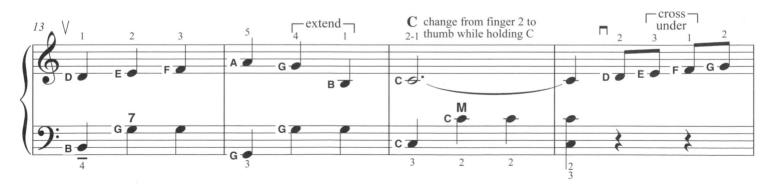

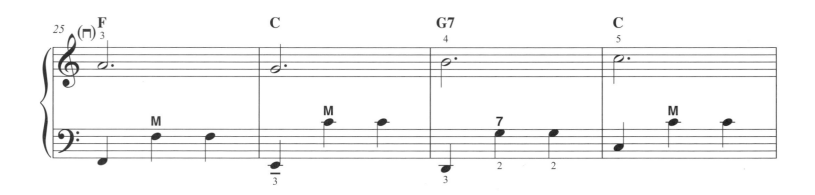

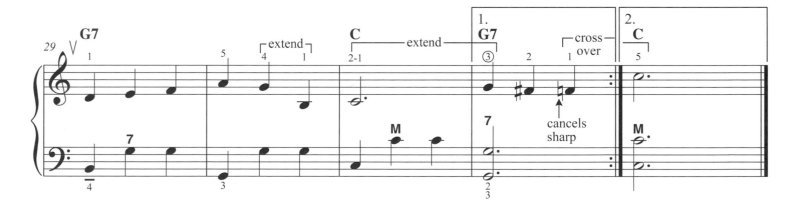

Contractions are the opposite of extensions. Often, the thumb is moved closer to a finger other than 2. Check out the following contractions in:

- "Beautiful Brown Eyes": measure 13, D-1 to F-4
- "Bingo": measure 4, A-4 to F-1; measure 16, B-4 to G-1
- "This Old Man": measure 12, F-1 to F♯-3

You will often see extensions and contractions, so be sure to read notes before you read the fingerings.

LESSON 14
ADVANCING CONCEPTS FOR BASS BUTTONS

Study this cadential (ending) pattern in the left hand. On count 2, play C and C major and you should find your fourth finger waiting very close to the F major chord. Find these on the bass buttons chart.

TRACK 77

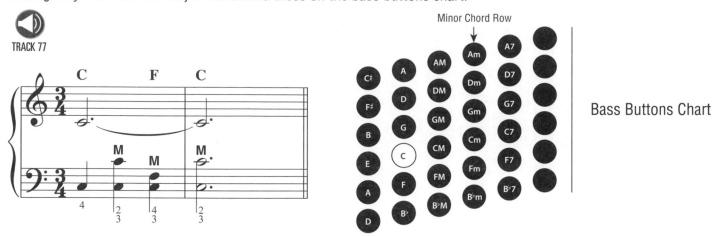

Bass Buttons Chart

Sometimes the right-hand melody and the left-hand accompaniment part will have pleasing duets. Study the bass buttons chart and find the B counterbass of G, the B♭, and A counterbass of F. Also, locate the F minor chord on the chart. Play with both hands the duets in the two examples below. Open the bellows a few inches before you start.

TRACK 78   **TRACK 79**

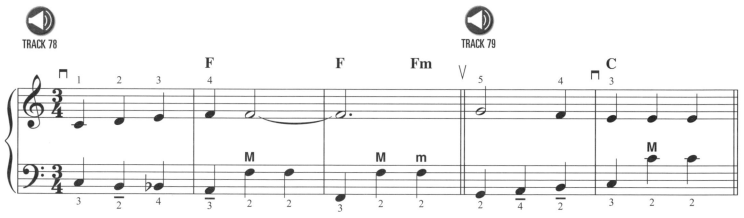

Fingerings are not always written in stone. When something is a bit tricky to play, it is worthwhile to try alternate solutions to find which is easier for you. Below are two finger suggestions for a bass button move. The first uses a fifth finger on C major, which is not too hard to find because the third finger has just played that C major chord. Using the fifth finger makes it easy to find the alternate bass A that precedes the D seventh chord. The intellectually easier, but physically "chancy," jump is illustrated in the second option using only fingers 3 and 2. Try both several times before you decide. Also, review the seventh chord row on the bass button chart above.

TRACK 80

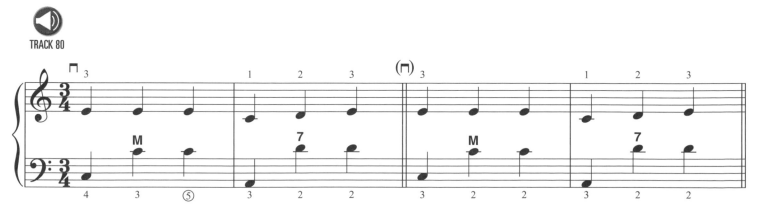

54

Notes to review for "Beautiful Brown Eyes"

B C D E F G A

BEAUTIFUL BROWN EYES

Traditional

TRACK 81

Practicing this last system extra times – hands separately, then together – will make it easier.

Do a thorough review of pages 50-55. Add any old tune (one) to your daily pleasure repertoire practice.

LESSON 15

F MAJOR SCALE for the Left Hand

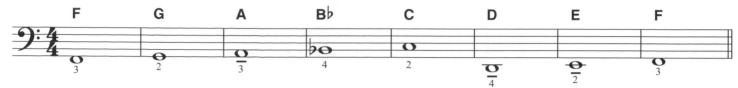

Scale notes always follow an alphabetical pattern, starting and ending with the letter name of the scale. Remember, bass buttons for single bass notes are written from low D to the second space C, so the note pattern will look a little different for each one. However, that will not affect the pattern of fingerings. Notice the *horizontal orientation* of Counterbass and Fundamental Bass rows.

Left-hand major scales are played using nearby bass buttons, from both the fundamental bass row and from the counterbass row. When you have learned the pattern for one major scale on the bass buttons, you have learned them all, because they follow exactly the same button pattern with exactly the same fingerings.

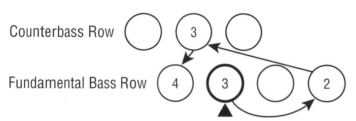

First half of Major Scale

Start the major scale with 3 in dark circle and follow the arrows.

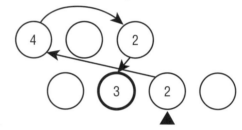

Second half of Major Scale

Continue the scale from the indicated 2 and again follow the arrows.

Key for new note
G♯ (measure 10)

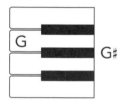

"Maori Farewell Song" has several interesting bass melodies, one of which comes directly from the left hand F major scale. However, check out measure 12 where the fifth finger plays the C button. This is reasonable since your third finger will have just played the D button; and following C, your fourth finger will play the B Counterbass above G. Practice this several times, and it will feel normal. It is a lovely piece, so you will probably want to spend the extra practice time for the wonderful reward of playing it.

MAORI FAREWELL SONG

TRACK 82

Traditional New Zealand Folksong

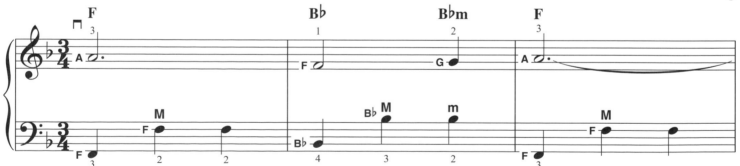

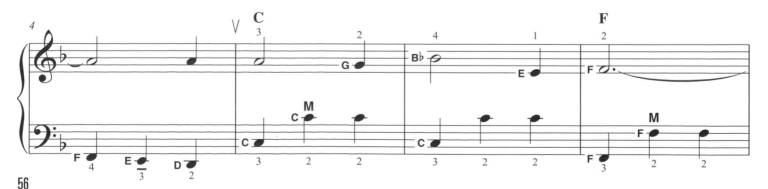

C MAJOR SCALE for the Left Hand

Learn the C major scale to prepare for "When the Saints Go Marching In." Review the bass buttons Major Scale pattern on the previous page.

LESSON 16

THE BASS CLEF NEIGHBORHOOD — "Friends and Family"

The fundamental row has been identified, so now we need to learn why these basses are called fundamental. The fundamental bass is the primary (fundamental) note that, with its "friends and family," provides the most pleasing sounds to accompany the melody.

Friends: Each bass note in the fundamental row has two "friends," other bass buttons that, when played in conjunction with the fundamental bass (F.B.), add musical interest to the accompaniment. The first is what we might call a "next door friend." This is identified as an alternate bass (A.B.); it also happens to be in the fundamental bass row. This button is just above the fundamental bass (toward your chin). (And, yes, it can also be a fundamental bass, with its own "friends and family." But don't worry about that right now.) We might say the other friend is one who "lives across the alley" in the counterbass row. Written as a note, it will always have a short line under it to identify it as a counterbass (Cb.). This counterbass is nearer the bellows and slightly down toward the floor. Find any fundamental bass and locate its alternate bass and counterbass. Play these three buttons in various patterns and become familiar with these sounds.

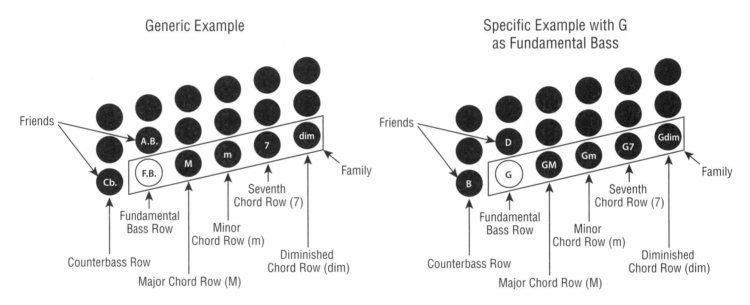

Family: Each fundamental bass has a "family" of four chords that use its letter name. G has a "family" consisting of G major, G minor, G seventh, and G diminished. You can see the rows for each of these chords on several of the bass charts; especially study the bass chord chart on page 80.

Letters above the grand staff, as below, tell you the "family" for the chord.

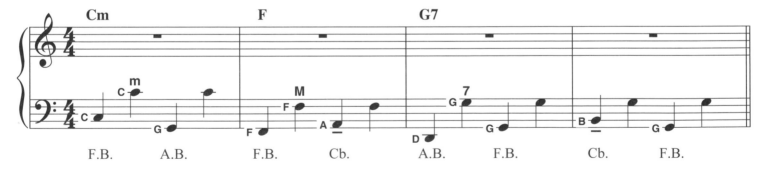

In the first measure, the chords are C minor; in the second measure, F major; the last two measures have G seventh chords, So, even though alternate basses or counterbasses are used, the chords are always determined by the letter above the grand staff.

Not all fundamental, alternating bass, and counterbass notation patterns look alike, just as not all bass scales look alike. However, reading the bass clef notes need not be tricky as long as you remember that, for accordion, the bass clef notes are always within a seven-note range. This never changes. So, D will be written the same place, be it a fundamental bass, an alternating bass, or a counterbass. F will always be just below the bass clef. G will always be on the lowest line of the bass clef, etc.

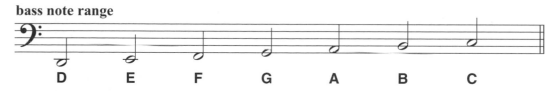

Below is a chart that shows many fundamental basses with counterbass and alternating bass "friends," always in that order – F.B., Cb., A.B. (The chart also shows notes of "family" chords for each fundamental bass.) You know some of these; others you may use later on. Observe the three patterns in which these "friends" are notated as they fit into the seven-note range. Play through all these patterns with major chords (use 3-2-3-2-3-2 fingering) and notice that you are *playing* the same pattern throughout. Try it also with seventh chords (use 4-2-4-2-3-2 fingering). Again, the *playing* patterns are always the same.

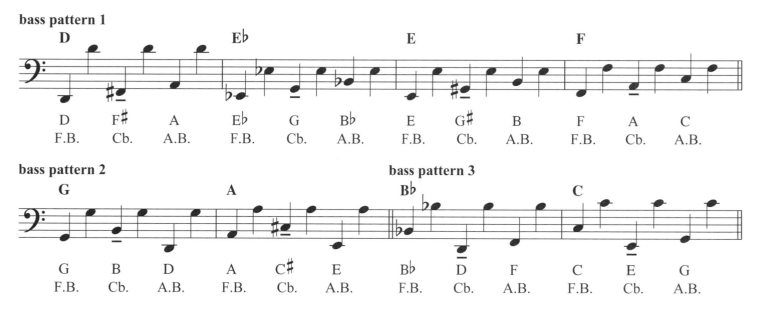

Perhaps you noticed that the chords also fall within their own seven-note range. It is reviewed below. These chords ("family"), whether major, minor, seventh, or diminished are notated from E to D.

Below are several combinations of basses/chords you will read in "When the Saints Go Marching In." Study each one and compare the basses and chords with the bass/chord chart on the last page, and examples above.

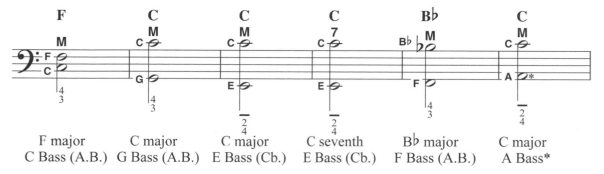

*A is the Counterbass of F, easily played with the fourth finger.

WHEN THE SAINTS GO MARCHING IN

By James M. Black

TRACK 83

Review and practice the F major scale, the C major scale, and learn the G major scale below. In your next several pieces, you will be playing bass solos that utilize significant portions of these bass scales. Also, "Bingo" uses all three key signatures of these scales.

G MAJOR SCALE for the Left Hand

LESSON 17

ANOTHER KEY SIGNATURE

The key of G major has one sharp, F♯. The F♯ in the key signature at the beginning of a song automatically turns all notes that "look like F" into F♯s. Be alert to this.

Key of G major
one sharp, F♯

Notice in the key signature above that the fifth line of the treble staff and fourth line of the bass staff intersect the center "parallelogram" (or slanted square) of the sharp. On the treble keyboard, F♯ is the black key immediately after the F key and nearer to the floor. Find the four F♯s on your keyboard. Play them.

While you will want to train yourself to be on the lookout for F♯s, *nevertheless you can predict where you will see them* on the clef. While they can be any place on the page, at this point in your studies, F♯ will either be in the first space or on the top line of the treble clef. See how easily you can find them in your music. On the bass clef F♯ will appear just below the lowest line. Review the G scale and, check "Skip to My Lou" (page 66, measure 4, fourth note), counterbass of D. As a chord, F♯ would appear on the fourth line.

Let's practice finding several other sharps on the keyboard to become accustomed to moving to the nearest black key in the direction of the floor when you see sharped notes:

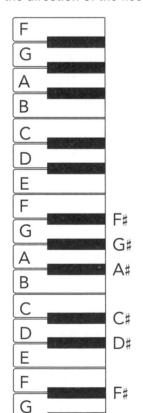

Can you find the F♯, C♯, G♯, D♯, higher F♯, and A♯ on the keyboard. The two F♯s need no signs in front of them, because they are already sharped by the key signature.

A natural sign (♮) cancels a sharp.

THREE KEY SIGNATURES — Three Major Scales (treble)

You have already learned to play the F major scale, the C major scale, and the G major scale with the left hand. These three scales are shown below in the treble clef for the right hand. Notice that the F major scale uses the fourth finger on B♭. The C major scale and G major scale share the exact same fingering. Be sure to use the fourth finger only on F♯ in the G major scale and only on B when you play the C major scale. If you like, you can read the notes and fingering backward and play the scales down as well as up.

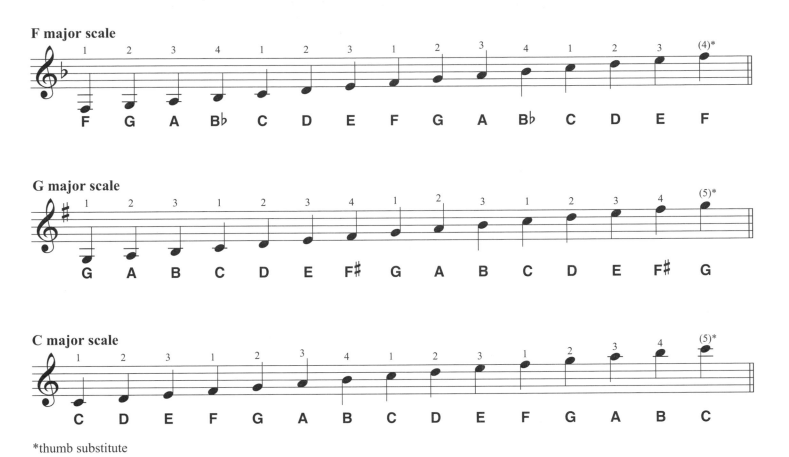

F major scale

G major scale

C major scale

*thumb substitute

Your next piece, "Bingo," has three key signatures. First, you will see the key of F major, followed by the key of G major in measure 13, and then C major in measure 25. Notice that in measure 12 there are four transitional eighth notes and after the double bar the B♭ is replaced with an F♯. Then, in measure 24, there are eighth notes leading to the melody in C major; the F♯ is cancelled and replaced with a natural sign since the key of C major has no sharps or flats.

Very important new piece of information: Sometimes a sharp or flat that is not in the key signature will occur within a piece. This sharp or flat is called an accidental. (Example: The F♯ in measure 12 of "Bingo.") This sharp in measure 12 of "Bingo" "has power" to sharp any following note that looks like F in that same measure. So, the notes in this measure are F–rest–F♯–D–E–F♯.

New Notation Format: Thus far, the note letter names have appeared in or beside the noteheads. From this point on, you will read notes with no "helps;" you will be reading standard notation on the remaining pieces and warm-ups. The three scales above provide a useful reference with more treble notes than you will read in the remainder of this book. Study these notes and refer to them as necessary. Bass clef notes are presented thoroughly on the pages entitled "Preparing to Read the Bass Clef," "More About Note Reading — Treble and Bass," as well as "Getting Around the Bass Clef Neighborhood — 'Friends and Family.'" Chord notes, of course, are easily recognized by the chord symbols written above the grand staff.

BINGO

Traditional

TRACK 84

Review pieces and concepts carefully and thoroughly, pages 50-65. Drop two older pieces, and add any two "not-so-old" pieces to your daily repertoire practice. Be sure to give extra practice time to "Maori Farewell Song," "When the Saints Go Marching In," and "Bingo" before you advance to the remaining six lessons. You have learned much!

LESSON 18

When you see *8va* - - - - ┐ over a group of notes, this means to play those same notes an octave (eight notes) higher.

SKIP TO MY LOU

Traditional

66

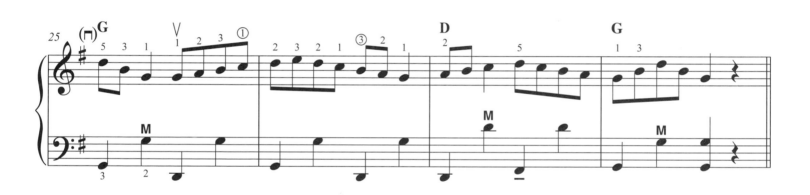

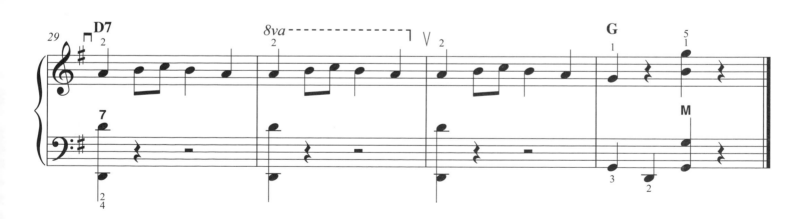

"Skip to My Lou" has an introduction in measures 1-4 and an extended ending in measures 29-32. These are set off by double bar lines after measures 4 and 28.

LESSON 19

Notice that this piece modulates
from F major to C major
in measures 12 to 13.

THIS OLD MAN

Traditional

A Note About "John Jacob Jingleheimer Schmidt"

Your next piece, "John Jacob Jingleheimer Schmidt," is a polka and is in 2/4 meter. There are two counts in each measure. A polka looks different from pieces in 4/4 meter because, while the quarter note is still the main pulse, the accompaniment is notated in eighth notes, as compared to the quarter-note accompaniment for many pieces in 4/4 meter. Also, with polkas, the characteristic style includes a lighter touch for the left-hand accompaniment, and the tempo is quicker than many types of pieces in 4/4 meter. Compare the two examples below. Other than the differences noted above, your fingers play exactly the same notes in both examples. By the way, as you review "Skip to My Lou," you might feel as if it seems like a polka... You may be on to something.

TRACK 87

LESSON 20

Conducting in $\frac{2}{4}$ meter

When an eighth note is written as a single note, it has a flag (no beams) that is always on the right side of the stem: ♪ ♪

TRACK 88

JOHN JACOB JINGLEHEIMER SCHMIDT

(open bellows a little with air button)

Traditional

Review the most recent four or five pieces. Add one to your repertoire.

LESSON 21

THE DOTTED-QUARTER NOTE*

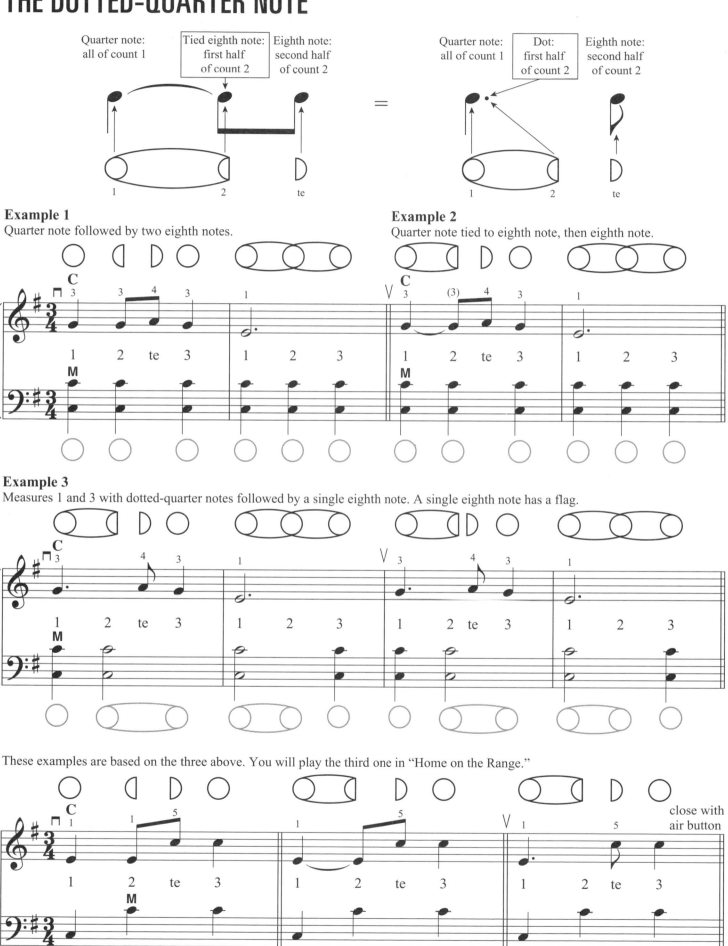

Example 1
Quarter note followed by two eighth notes.

Example 2
Quarter note tied to eighth note, then eighth note.

Example 3
Measures 1 and 3 with dotted-quarter notes followed by a single eighth note. A single eighth note has a flag.

These examples are based on the three above. You will play the third one in "Home on the Range."

* Adapted from *Piano ABC's Level One* and Patent No. US 7,453,036 B1, used by permission.

HOME ON THE RANGE

By Dan Kelly

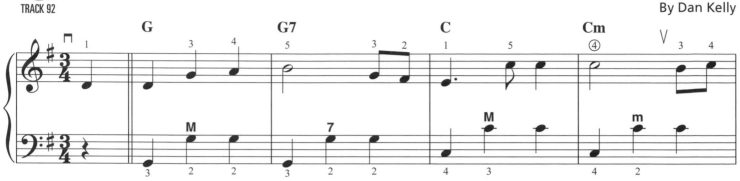

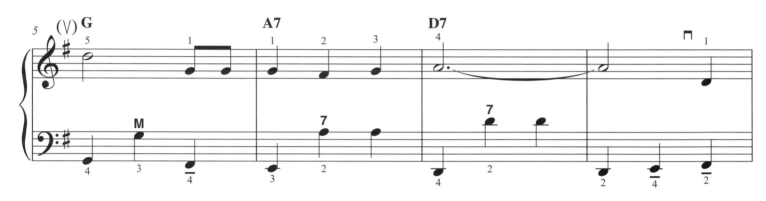

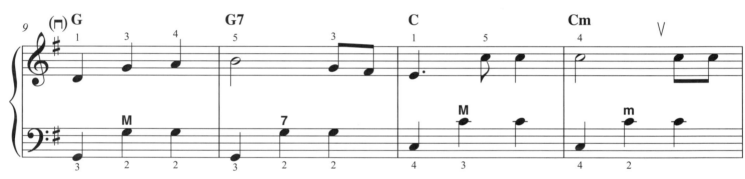

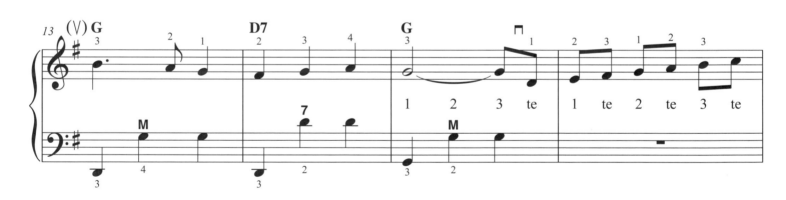

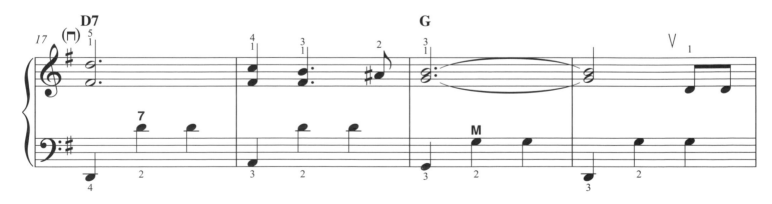

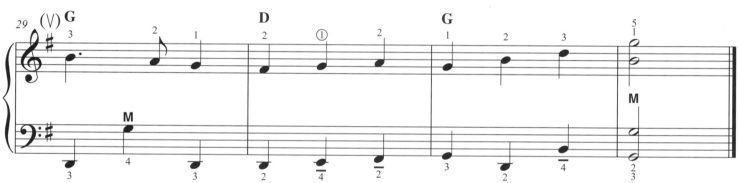

An important reminder: In measure 22 of "Home on the Range," the sharp sign, an accidental, has "power" to turn all three notes that look like C into C♯s. It's "power" ends at the bar line between measures 22 and 23. The natural sign (♮) in measure 23 is not really necessary, but is a friendly reminder.

LESSON 22
WARM-UP STUDIES FOR "GREENSLEEVES"

Read and play the following notes for the introduction of "Greensleeves." The first set of notes occurs on the first system. Several of the higher- and middle-range notes combine on the second system.

higher-range notes   middle-range notes

B   A   G   F#   E   D   D#   C   B   A   G   F#

Here are two examples of fingerings (circled) in which the second finger has stepped over the thumb; the thumb held its note until this smooth move was complete. The third finger has quietly let go as the fourth finger stepped to its next note, together with the second finger. Also, study the descending line of lower notes in the example to the right, beginning with the first E, then C, next B, A, and finally G, the second white key from your chin.

Practice this right-hand passage until it is comfortably easy to prepare for both hands (in measures 29–32), in which the bass part is just a little tricky.

Practice this bass solo, which uses buttons only from the fundamental bass row.

As you practice these bass patterns, remember that the C and E basses have rhinestones or creases. Feel C with your fifth finger and/or E with your third finger as you learn these patterns.

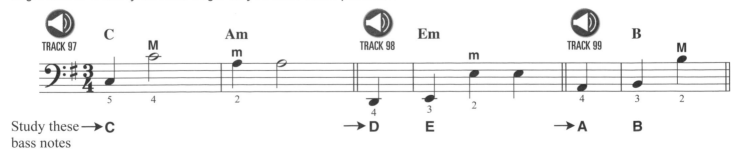

Study these → C   → D   E   → A   B
bass notes

74

Bass Chart
for "Greensleeves" and
"Cockles and Mussels"

Italian

(*piano*) *p* – soft: Pull or push bellows with less pressure

(*mezzo forte*) *mf* – medium loud: Pull or push bellows with
more pressure

(*forte*) *f* – loud: Pull or push bellows with still more pressure

TRACK 100

GREENSLEEVES

Traditional English Folksong

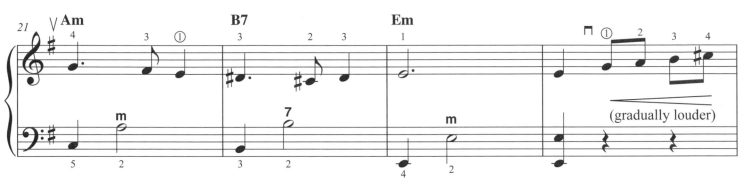

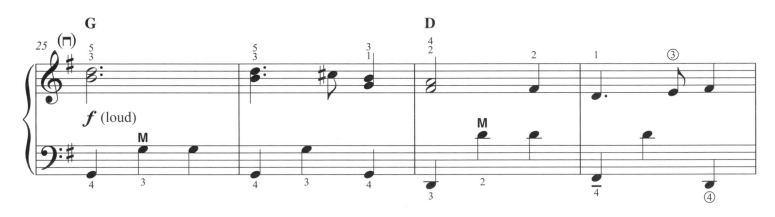

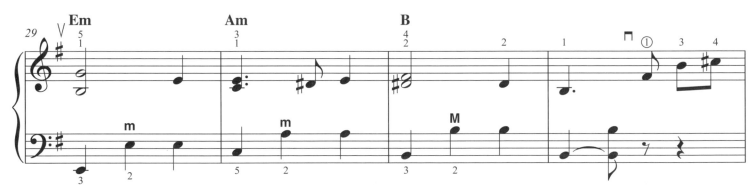

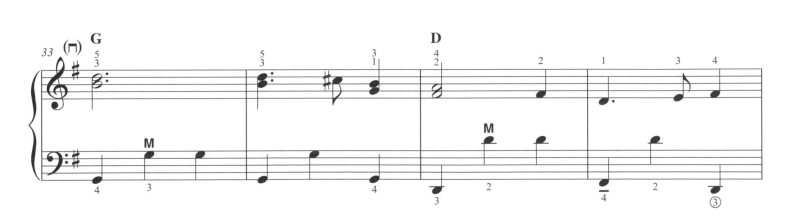

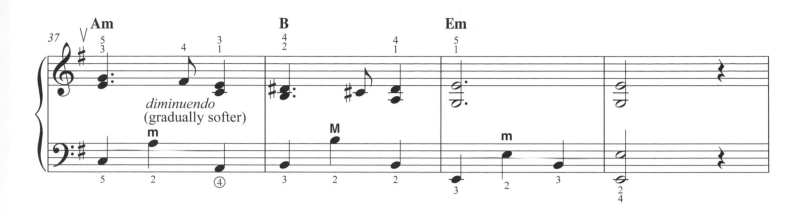

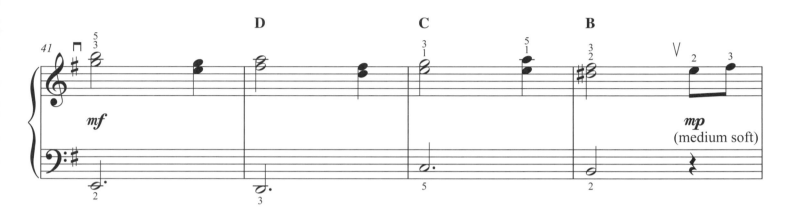

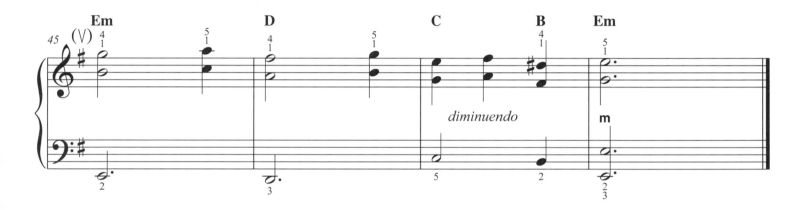

Study and practice the bass part for "Cockles and Mussels" on this first system.

Then add the chords with these same basses as written below.

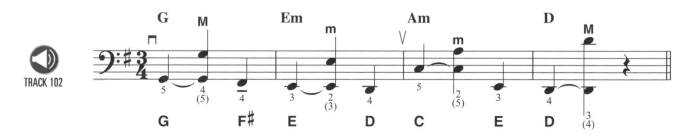

LESSON 23

COCKLES AND MUSSELS
(Molly Malone)

Traditional Irish Folksong

TRACK 103

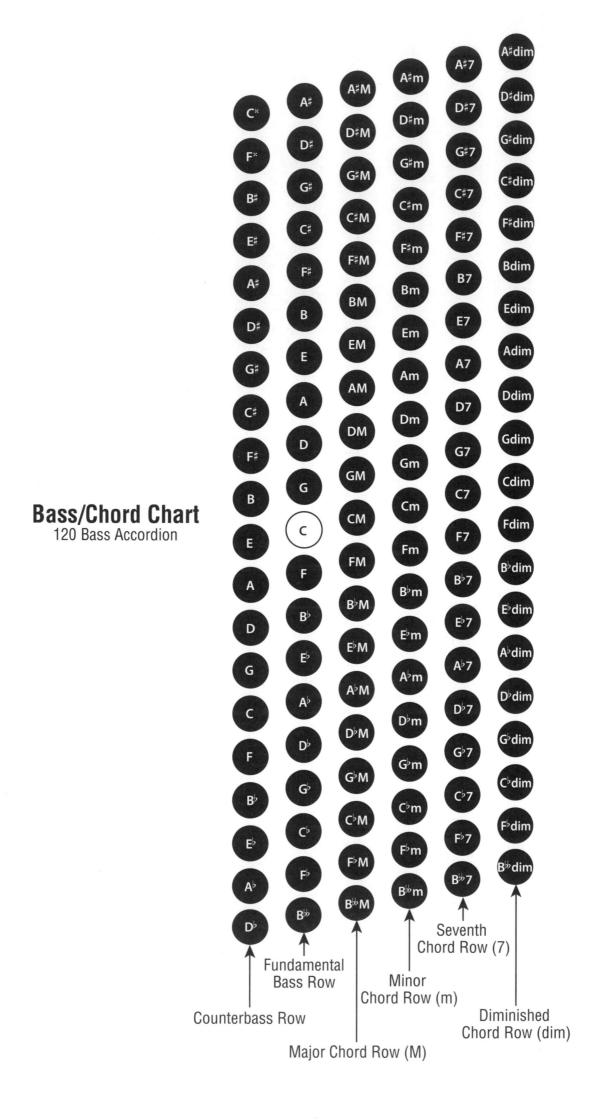

Bass/Chord Chart
120 Bass Accordion

Counterbass Row

Fundamental Bass Row

Major Chord Row (M)

Minor Chord Row (m)

Seventh Chord Row (7)

Diminished Chord Row (dim)